# SERMONS ON ACTS 16

Compiled by
**Stanley Barnes**

AMBASSADOR

BELFAST, NORTHERN IRELAND
GREENVILLE, USA

Sermons on Acts 16
© Copyright 2001 Stanley Barnes

ISBN 1  84030  100  7


*Ambassador Publications*
a division of
Ambassador Productions Ltd.
Providence House
Ardenlee Street,
Belfast,
BT6 8QJ
Northern Ireland
www.ambassador-productions.com

Emerald House
427 Wade Hampton Blvd.
Greenville
SC 29609, USA
www.emeraldhouse.com

# INTRODUCTION

In this our third book in the series of sermons on favourite texts of the Bible, we once again bring together famous preachers who through their writings and sermons, have been a wonderful blessing to ministers of the gospel down through the years. Preachers such as D. L. Moody, T. Dewitt Talmage, Charles Finney, R. A. Torrey and C. H. Spurgeon, all from different doctrinal backgrounds, but seeking to expound the Word of God in answer to what continues to be one of the greatest questions of all time.

*What must I do to be saved?*

The inclusion of these preachers in this volume is not an endorsement of everything they have said or written, but I believe the aim of these great men of God was to preach Christ with compassion and love to those who are still seeking the way of salvation just as the Philippian jailor was almost 2000 years ago.

Stanley Barnes
March 2001

# CONTENTS

# WILLIAM PATTESON NICHOLSON

∽

The Rev. William Patteson Nicholson or W.P. as he was affectionately known was one of Ulster's best-known evangelists. Born just outside Bangor, Northern Ireland, he left school at fifteen and went to sea as an apprentice. On a trip home to see his mother he came under great conviction while sitting at the fireside. A voice spoke within urging him to repent of his sin and to quote his own words, 'Suddenly and powerfully I was saved.' He then studied at the Bible Training Institute in Glasgow after which he became the evangelist for the Lanarkshire Christian Union. In 1908 he joined Chapman and Alexander in their missions in Australia and America, returning to America to settle with his family. As a result of his United Gospel Campaigns in the early 1920's in the North of Ireland, thousands were brought to Christ. Converts came from every section of the community, Protestants, Catholics, publicans and drunkards; gunmen and thieves; religious churchgoers and down and outs; all knelt before God in repentance, confessing their need of Christ and crying for mercy. Dr. W. Graham Scroggie said of him, 'They may say what they like about Nicholson but after all the test of a man's work and words is the goods he delivers - and he has delivered the goods.' This sermon was preached at the 1925 Keswick Convention in England.

# Chapter One

# WHAT MUST I DO TO BE SAVED?

∽

*And brought them out, and said, Sirs, what must I do
to be saved? - Acts 16:30*

∽

Where I come from in the North of Ireland (Bangor), by the seaside, during the summer time, we have open-air meetings, so that the people who go there for the health of their body may have an opportunity of finding the Lord Jesus Christ as their personal Saviour. One Sunday night I was standing on a three-legged stool speaking, and I put my hand on a man's shoulder - I saw that he had been deeply interested during the open-air service and I said, "Well, friend, are you a saved man?" "Leave me alone: I'm tired and sick to death with you preachers!" "That's not answering my question." "Well, you might come along the shore and we will talk things over." He said he originally came from Bangor, and had gone out to Canada with his parents as a little child, and had been an elder for thirty-three years in a Presbyterian church. He went on: "I have heard sermons all my life on salvation, the joy of salvation, the power and blessing of salvation, and many times I have been urged to receive salvation, because it would be necessary not only for my present good, but for my eternal welfare. You are a Presbyterian minister. Well, let me say that I have never heard any minister telling me how to get what I ought to have." I hung my head in shame. Because we have been brought up in a Christian country it is expected that everybody is familiar with the way in which to be saved. When you want to join a church, you get into a confirmation or some other class before you enter the church, and you expect something to happen, and somehow or another it is taken as a matter of course that, because you have had experience and knowledge, the heart is alright. You enter into fellowship with the church and go to the Lord's table, but there never has taken place in your life a real, radical, revolutionary change; you have never been "born again." Because of the position you occupy in the church you are shy and timid about making your need known. Many a time you have come to a convention like this in the hope that some word, dropped "by the wayside" might be the means of leading you to the Lord Jesus Christ. But again and again you have gone back disappointed because you are in perplexity and difficulty regarding this matter of salvation. We Presbyterians are not very ready somehow or another to declare what we have discerned as our common experience. We are shy and reserved.

## ORTHODOX PRESBYTERIAN

I was brought up in a strict, orthodox Presbyterian home, where we did not flippantly speak of these things of the soul. They were spoken about on Sunday, but during the rest of the week we never heard another word about them. If I could only have made my needs known to those I came in contact with, I should have been saved years before I was. I was anxious and perplexed about the matter, but did not know how salvation was to be got; I knew nothing of how to come to the Lord Jesus Christ and accept Him as my personal Saviour. I am taking it for granted that there may be such a one here in this tent tonight, one brought up in a religious home and environment, with a good standing in your church, and yet you do not know Jesus Christ as your personal Saviour. How are you to be saved? I want to make it as clear as I can. You may not like what I say, but I guarantee you will understand every word I say before I am done. It is a very short time till the place that knows us will know us no more forever. God only knows how soon some of us will be in the presence of the King, and if you are not saved tonight you may be in Hell as long as God lives.

## FIRST

In the first place, you must acknowledge that you are not saved, that you are a lost, guilty, "condemned already" sinner. In spite of your respectability and morality, you are a sinner without hope, without God, a stranger to "the covenant of promise," without strength. How deplorable your position is. May the Lord open your eyes tonight to see how lost and ruined you are outside the Lord Jesus Christ. If you are to know Christ and His saving grace, that is the first thing you have to come to "Lord, I am not saved; I am a guilty, lost sinner, born," it may be, "of godly parents, brought up in a godly home, having lived a respectable and upright life, but unsaved; never having been washed in the Blood, or been born of the Spirit of God." Are you willing to take that place? That is the hardest job that the preacher or the Spirit of God has - to get men and women to that place. We want to maintain our integrity before God, and tell God what wonderful lives we are living and what wonderful people we are. When we look round on an audience like this, what a variety of people there are. In God's sight there are only two classes - saved, and unsaved. It does not matter whether you are rich, or poor, or a drunkard, or a sober man, or vulgar in your vice, or cultured and refined in your vice. You are still an unsaved man or woman in the sight of God. Are you willing to take the place that God puts us all in? The Gospel levels the whole crowd of us. It does not matter whether you are King George or a poor murderer in gaol today. We are all in one pew. Whether you are a woman wearing white kid gloves and clothed in scarlet, or whether you are the cleanest man, you are put by God in the same pew with the worst people who have ever lived. "For all have sinned and come short of the glory of God." There may be degrees in that fact, but the fact remains regarding every man and woman outside Jesus Christ.

## SECOND

You must also acknowledge that you can never do anything to save yourself. I hope you will not think me irreverent when I say that if God has asked me to make a plan of salvation which would have suited, I could have done it. It would not have offended sinful men and women. If anyone preaches a gospel that does not offend, it is not the Gospel of Christ. I do not know anything more offensive to the religious, cultured, intellectual man than the Gospel. "Not of works lest any man should boast." You may be baptised, confirmed, or take the Lord's Supper, but it is "not of works." You may never have done a wrong thing so far as you know, and lived as clean and straight a life as a natural man or woman, but you will never merit anything in God's sight. You cannot get God under obligation. You cannot say, "Lord, you see how I have lived, what a lot of good I have done, what a lot of money I have given; you know all the prayers I have offered, and how regularly I have been to my church. Surely you do not put me in the same place with the drunkard, or the blaspheming man or woman?" Yes, just the same. That is what makes it hard to get religious, respectable men and women to take God's salvation. You have got to acknowledge that your good works are nothing but a pile of manure in God's sight, your self-righteousness nothing but filthy rags. It did not bother me very much to get saved along that line, for the Lord in His sovereign grace allowed the Devil to strip me of everything, and one was glad to take salvation on those terms. But some of you have been respectable, nice people; very kind, amiable, religious, devout. To some of you my remarks may come as a kind of shock. When you are told that your good works count for nothing in God's sight, and that your self-righteousness is nothing but filthy rags, your back gets up and you get angry, and you say, "Now look here, I want you to know to whom you are talking, and who my father and mother were, and how I was educated." The Lord says, "I do not bother My head about that. You must acknowledge that you cannot do anything to save your soul or to merit or deserve salvation."

## NONSENSE

I was talking to a Belfast businessman, a nice fellow, after an open-air meeting, and I said, "Now what about this?" "You are talking a lot of nonsense!" "Will you tell me where the nonsense comes in?" "You know me?" "Yes, I have known you from a boy." "You know how religious I am. I am an elder in the church; I have lived a good life; my word is as good as my bond; I stand for integrity and morality in my business." I knew it to be true. "How generous I am!" I knew that to be true. "Will all this not count with God?" "It will sink you deeper in Hell unless you have got Christ." "Do you think I have got to come like a drunkard?" "Yes, just in the same way." "Like a harlot?" "Just in the same way." There are no fifty ways to Christ. He says, "I am the Way," and it is by the narrow way and the straight gate for all of us. We are not saved because we deserve salvation, but because we need it. "Not of works lest any man should boast." Supposing you got to heaven on the grounds of what you are as a natural man, and the life you are living, what a rebuff to some of us poor sinners! You would be strutting about like a peacock, and I want to tell you that you would spoil heaven for us poor Calvinistic sinners saved by grace. It is not of works, but on the ground of grace undeserved, unmerited favour.

## BIG DEVILS

On Saturday my mother would go and do shopping at a place some three miles away. There were no motors or electric cars in those days. She had seven children, and the girls were nearly as "big devils" as the boys. She did not know whether the house would be a house when she got back. But we had a girl in the house named Sally, and Sally could hit harder than any woman I have ever come across. Mother would say, "Sally, see that the boys and girls behave themselves till I come back." And she did. When Sally took the reins of government, it was pure undiluted law. When mother returned she would say, "How did they behave?" "They behaved well." Then mother would take from a parcel something and say, "James, because you were such a good boy there's a wee present." "Sarah, because you were such a good girl, there's a wee present for you." "Willie, because you were such a good boy there's a wee present for you also." I didn't buy what mother gave me, but because I was good I got my mother's wee present.

I do not think there ever was a day when the Devil was deceiving and deluding the minds of sinning men and women about salvation like the present. There are innumerable multitudes of men and women thronging the highway to Hell, hoping that by heaping up all sorts of good works, God will meet them in grace and save their souls. No, on the authority of God's Word you and I will never merit salvation. We must acknowledge.

Nothing in my hand I bring,
Simply to Thy Cross I cling.
Not the labour of my hands
Can fulfil Thy law's demands;
Could my zeal no respite know,
Could my tears forever flow,
All for sin could not atone;
Thou must save, and Thou alone.

How flippantly we sing it, and yet how it strikes at the very foundation of what some of you are building on for time and eternity. Jesus Christ came not to call the righteous; He came to call sinners, He came to seek and to save lost men and women. If you will not acknowledge that you are lost, that you are unrighteous, that you are a sinner, you can never deserve or merit salvation.

## THIRD

The third thing is, you must be willing to abandon yourself entirely to Jesus Christ, to belong to Christ, spirit, soul and body.

Were the whole realm of nature mine,
That were an offering far too small;

Love so amazing, so Divine,
Demands-
*What does it demand?*
My soul, my life, my all!

I hear some people say today, "You do not need to do anything, or to give up anything to get salvation." What do you mean by believing on Christ? *Belonging* to Him. "His name shall be called Jesus, for He shall save" - anybody? No, He is not on that job. "He shall save HIS people," and if you are not willing to be His you will never have His salvation. You must think the Lord Jesus is a poor fool to save you and let you serve the Devil just as much as you like. Whenever you come to Christ you have got to say, "Lord, I am a guilty, lost, hopeless, undone, condemned-already sinner; but, Lord, I am ready to be Thine alone;

O Lamb of God, I come.

Some people think that the Lord Jesus Christ is a short cut to Heaven, or a kind of fire-escape to get to Heaven; and that the Church of Christ is a kind of fire insurance institution, and that as long as they put their halfpenny in the plate every Sunday, and look pious, they will be safe from being sent to Hell, for by-and-by they will pull out their insurance policy and say, "I am insured!" The Lord never saves any man to keep him out of Hell; He saves him to take Hell out of him, and to make him holy, that he may serve God in righteousness and holiness all the days of his life. I do not know anything that would make salvation more popular, even if it were by grace, than if the Lord said, "You can dance as much as you like; you can gamble, and curse, and swear, and live like the Devil, and whenever you die I will take your soul to Heaven." There would be a lot of you on that job.

## AUSTRALIA

I was preaching in Freemantle (Australia), and at the end of the service I invited any who were anxious to come right up to the front, and I would deal with them personally and publicly. To one man who came up I said, "You are a lost sinner?" "Yes." "Are you willing to give up everything and come to Christ?" "No." "Then what are you doing here?" "I love with all my heart to put odds on horses, and do you think I'm going to give that up to get salvation? I'm away. Good night!" A young ruler said to the Master, "What must I do to have eternal life?" and Jesus said, "Sell all that thou hast." Dr. Hudson Taylor used to say, "Christ will not be Lord at all if He is not Lord of all." If you are not willing to break with the Devil for "Ye cannot serve God and mammon" - if you are not willing to renounce the world and to deny yourself, Jesus Christ cannot save you. He can only save those who are willing to acknowledge their guilty and lost condition, and are willing to be His and His alone for time and eternity. The story is told of Lord Nelson, that when he had defeated the French in battle, the French admiral was brought to his vessel, and he marched out on to the quarterdeck to Nelson, and in his French suavity made as if to shake hands with him. Nelson, who had only one hand, put it behind him and said, "Sir, it is your sword I want; not your hand." When you come to Jesus Christ that is what He says. "Hands up! Cease your rebellion, give in, give up here and now!" That is a hard thing. We are willing to give our money, we are willing to give a lot of our time. But to say, "Lord, everything in my boots and under my hair is yours for time and eternity"- that is a different thing. You have got to abandon yourself to Jesus Christ, spirit, soul and body. You cannot dictate terms to Him. After you have given yourself over to Him, you cannot tell Him you are going to Africa, or China, or wherever it may be. You cannot tell Him whether you will smoke tobacco, or play football, golf, or tennis. One is your Master when you become Christ's; He becomes Lord and Master of the life He redeems with His precious Blood. Unless you are willing to have the mastership of Christ, there is no salvation for you, however conscious you may be of your guilt and lost condition. During the Boer War I was out in South Africa, and after Lord Roberts had cleaned things up they sent Lord Kitchener out to make the thing real. Lord Kitchener got a British steel band around the enemy at Magersfontein, and he said, "I will give you three days to think this thing out, and if you do not I will tell you why!" On the third day there came forward from the enemy someone with a white flag and a document, which said, "These are the terms on which we are willing to accept peace." Said Kitchener, "I'm not here to talk of peace; I'm here to demand unconditional surrender; otherwise I will fight you." That is exactly the demand Christ makes. You cannot say, "Lord, I want to be saved, but to remain decent; I do not want to lose my reputation amongst my friends; I want to be respected as a Church of England member." I thank God, brother Presbyterians, that you cannot denominationalise Christ; you cannot make Christ an Episcopalian, or a Presbyterian, or a Methodist, or a Congregationalist, or a Baptist, or anything else denominationally. If you dictate to Christ and say, "Lord Jesus, this is what I have got to be, and how I am going to live, and what pleasures I am going to indulge in," that kind of thing has got to end. Every mouth must be stopped before Him.

To be Thine, yea, Thine alone,
O Lamb of God, I come.

## FOURTH

Fourth, you have got to ask the Lord to save you. If you are too proud to open your mouth now, there is a day coming when you will do it. The rich men, and kings, and the great men of the world - there is coming a day when they will cry upon the mountains and rocks to hide them from the wrath of the Lamb. Thank God, this is a day of grace, and there is a throne of grace, and we can come to the throne of grace and there find grace to help in time of need. Are you humble enough to ask Him? It is a hard thing to ask, especially if you have a lot of pride about you. I myself did not mind saying, "O God, as a dirty, guilty sinner, save me" - that stuck! How you would like if somehow the Lord would save you in your sleep, or at some other time when you are not thinking about it. But He saves you at your request. "Whosoever shall call on the name of the Lord shall be saved." It is not a matter of saying prayers; it is a matter of praying. There is all the difference in the world between these two things. I was saying prayers for twenty-three years, and going to Hell sixty minutes in the hour. But one morning, twenty-six years ago, I prayed at my mother's fireside; there I prayed for the first time in my life, and I got saved.

## A THEOLOGICAL STUDENT

There was a young fellow, a theological student, who could say he was brought up in Gamaliel's theological seminary, and he said, "According to the law blameless. I am an Israelite, of the tribe of Benjamin; I am zealous." He was first-rate at prayers. But, notwithstanding all that, he at last was constrained to cry out, "Lord, what wilt Thou?" In Heaven I can imagine God saying to the angels, "Hush! Behold he prayeth." "But, Lord, that is Saul of Tarsus. That fellow has been doing nothing else but being religious and saying prayers." "I never heard him till this time," says God. Has the Lord ever heard you? You may have murdered theology when you were at it; but has He heard you? A big divine in America went to Boston, and next morning they had it in the papers that it was the greatest prayer Boston ever heard. I wonder did God hear it? You can put up such a nice wee one. One would think that angel wings were coming out of your shoulder blades, judging by the way you look - everything so orderly, so regular! Have you ever cried out of the anguish of your heart, out of the depth of your need, as a guilty, lost sinner, "Jesus, save me, I perish; God, be merciful to me a sinner." So many people are like the Pharisee. When he came into the church he got a looking-glass and put it up, and said, "God, I" - "How do you do?" - "I thank Thee I am not like other men"; and he smiled at himself, "I give tithes of all I possess, I give things to the poor, I fast twice a week." Perhaps it saved him from dyspepsia and religious nausea. Jesus said, "The poor publican would not so much as lift his eyes to heaven, but smote upon his breast, saying, God, be merciful to me a sinner," and that man went down justified more than the other. He does not call him a man; He said "the other." Is that the kind of praying you do? "Lord, I hope you saw what a good person I am. Did you see that sixpence I gave to that blind man? And I gave five pounds to my church." God does not hear that. Have you come to the Lord, and, out of a broken and contrite heart, said, "Lord, save me?" Maybe it is a timid cry, with a sob, or the dropping of a tear, but it is a cry that God will hear.

### FIFTH

Fifth. Here is the crux. Take what He offers you. "Lord, I accept Thee as my Saviour, I trust Thee with my soul," and as surely as God is in His sky above, you are a saved man or woman. "What things soever ye desire when ye pray, believe that ye receive them, and," says, God, "I will see that you have them." You say to your child, or daughter, or son, "When Christmas comes I'm going to give you a present," and the child has as good as got it, and says, "My father is going to give me a beautiful doll, or a wheelbarrow, or a cricket bat." You pledge yourself to keep your word. "What things soever ye desire when ye pray, believe that ye receive them, and ye shall have them." Take that for granted, and you will not be long on the road until in your heart you will know you have the grace of God and salvation. Charlotte Elliott had been brought into the fellowship of the Church at Easter. Her godly minister thought she was truly converted and that her soul rested on Christ. One day he was going past where she lived, and she was coming out of her house dressed for a ball and stepped into a carriage. The old man nearly dropped on seeing that, and he went quickly before the carriage door was closed, and said, "Charlotte, are you saved?" She banged the door and got away from the old man, but she did not get away from his question. Instead of dancing till daylight, she was home before midnight, and for a long week her pride was dying. At last she could stand it no more, and she started to seek the minister. As she was making her way to where he lived, she met him on the street, and she said, "I'm delighted to see you. I was making my way to your home, and I have come for two things. First, I apologise to you for my rudeness." "That's all right, Charlotte; I understand it." "Sir, how am I to answer that question you asked me?" "Charlotte," he said, "just as you are, come to Christ." Just as she was she came to Christ, and some time afterwards she wrote these beautiful words which have been the means of leading thousands to Him:-

Just as I am without one plea,
But that Thy blood was shed for me,
And that Thou bidd'st me come to Thee,
O Lamb of God, I come.

Just as I am and waiting not,
To rid my soul of one dark blot,
To Thee, Whose blood can cleanse each spot,
O Lamb of God, I come.

That is the way you have got to come, that is the way we have all
got to come, and you may come right now, just as you are, for "Him
that cometh to Me I will in no wise cast out."

# JOHN WILBUIR CHAPMAN

John Wilbur Chapman was a Presbyterian minister and evangelist born in Richmond, Indiana. At the tender age of four his favourite pastime was standing on a chair, which to him was a pulpit, and playing the role of a preacher. The son of godly parents and greatly influenced by their spiritual example he was soon led to accept Christ by his Sunday school teacher. He graduated from Lake Forest College and Lane Seminary, Cincinnati and he was ordained in 1882. He held pastorates in four different states, but devoted most of his ministry to evangelism, working alongside D.L. Moody and Charles M. Alexander. His evangelistic tours took him all over the world and he won many souls for the Lord in his campaigns. He was also the first director of Winona Lake Bible Conference and in 1917 his church's general assembly elected him as its moderator.

He also authored many books, which were a great influence to believers encouraging them to have a deeper devotion to Christ. Among them were *Ivory Palaces of the King; Revivals and Missions; Present-Day Evangelism; Another Mile* and *When Home is Heaven.* This sermon is taken from his book *'Revival Sermons'.*

Chapter Two

# THE ANXIOUS SOUL'S QUESTION

☙

*And brought them out, and said, Sirs, what must I do*
*to be saved? And they said, Believe on the Lord Jesus Christ,*
*and thou shalt be saved, and thy house.* - Acts 16:30,31.

☙

The apostle Paul lived in a state of perpetual revival. He had only to come into Philippi, the principal city of Macedonia, and to sit by the riverbank, and Lydia, the seller of purple, straightway believed and was baptized. He had only to walk along the streets to the place of prayer, and there was so much of power about him that "a certain damsel, possessed with the spirit of divination," followed him and cried, saying, "These men are the servants of the most high God," and "Paul being grieved, turned and said to the spirit, I command thee in the name of Jesus Christ to come out of her. And he came out the same hour. And when her masters saw that the hope of their gains was gone, they caught Paul and Silas and drew them into the market place," tore off their clothes, beat them with many stripes and cast them into an inner prison, fastening their feet in the stocks. But this did not in any way affect these servants of God. It was doubtless true in their case, as one of the modern poets has expressed it, that "stone walls do not a prison make, nor iron bars a cage," for at midnight, in the midst of all the darkness, they "sang praises unto God: and the prisoners heard them." What a strange sound it must have been in the old jail, where ordinarily only curses had been heard! But suddenly there came a great earthquake; the foundations of the prison began to shake and the doors were thrown open and "every one's bands were loosed." In the midst of all this confusion, the jailor sprang into their presence, and was ready to kill himself, thinking the prisoners had escaped, when Paul exclaimed, "Do thyself no harm: for we are all here."

## 'CONVICTION' THE FIRST STEP

There is just in this connection a clear distinction drawn between men of influence and men of power. Ordinarily we say, what the church needs today is men of influence, meaning by this men of position. And so it does; but from this illustration I think we may argue, the greater demand is for men of power. Paul and Silas had not influence enough to keep themselves out of jail, but they had a power sufficient to pray down the prison walls and throw wide open its doors. There is also in the whole incident given to us a true and striking picture of what it means for one to be saved.

If I were an artist, I should like to draw upon a blackboard a great letter "C," then fill out from that one letter four words. These four words would present to us a picture of this Philippian jailor not only, but also of the one who really and truly comes to Christ. The first word would be *"Conviction."* This we surely find in the jailor, for we are told he "came trembling." It is not possible for any one to be saved without first of all experiencing real conviction; however, it ought to be suggested that in different individuals it may manifest itself in different ways.

First. Sometimes it is evidenced in great need. One would display his ignorance if he were to assert that Nicodemus, for example, was the chief of sinners; for he was a ruler of his people, an honored member of the Sanhedrin, a most circumspect man in every way; but in his heart there was a great sense of his need, which his position had never satisfied; and this compelled him, I imagine, to seek out the Great Teacher.

Second. Not infrequently it may assume the form of a sense of complete unworthiness, such as the poor publican had when he said, "God be merciful to me a sinner;" but the article there in the Greek was a definite one, and what he really said was this: "God be merciful to me the sinner," as if he were the only one in the world. This is a most hopeful condition.

Third. As a rule, it is the consciousness that we have sinned and are, therefore, under condemnation that disturbs us; and in the unregenerate state, it is the fearfulness that the penalty of the broken law may fall upon us; yet I am quite clear in my own mind that there may be a deeper conviction of one's sins after one's regeneration than before.

Stanley tells us that he found men in Africa who never knew that they were black until they looked upon a white man. So many a man can never know what sin is until he sees it in the presence of Jesus Christ. But whatever the form of conviction, it must surely be experienced before the light will dawn. Come to Him just as you are, for He can satisfy your longings by filling you with Himself and He is able to blot out all your transgressions and forgive all your sins.

## 'CONTRITION' THE NEXT ESSENTIAL

The second word starting with the letter "C" would be *"Contrition."* This the Philippian jailor had, for he "fell down" before them. It is certainly true that one cannot come to God unless, first of all, he be possessed of the broken and contrite heart. Why should this not be true? We have sinned against God and there must be contrition for it if we are to be forgiven. God may be ever so willing to forgive, still He does not do it without contrition.

In the State prison of Iowa there is a young man held as a convict, against whom the charge of arson stands, and also the attempt to kill. Very recently, the party whose building was fired circulated a petition asking that the young man be pardoned; the man whose life was attempted followed his example, and succeeded in securing the name of the judge, by whom he was sentenced, the attorney who prosecuted him, and the entire jury which found him guilty. This petition was carried to the Governor. In the face of it, strong as it was, he said, "No, the man cannot be pardoned; for," said he "his crime was not committed against the individual, but against the commonwealth of Iowa, and he must serve his sentence." And it ought to be remembered by the sinner that these words are true, "Against thee and thee only have I sinned." So there must be contrition or there cannot be salvation; and yet what a marvelous thing it is that, if one be ever so great a sinner, the moment this spirit is manifest God blots out all his transgressions.

It is stated that, in St. Petersburg, a father's heart was well-nigh broken because of the prodigality of his son who was addicted to the habit of gambling, and with that came the accompanying vices. At last the old father conceived the idea that what the boy needed was better surroundings, and so he set out to secure them. What a mistake this is and how many have made it! That is not what you need. This father of whom I speak secured his son's appointment in the army, but he went from bad to worse until he had reached the end of it all.

Completely discouraged, he was casting up his accounts and, when the overwhelming sum was known, in great desperation he wrote at the bottom of the column these words, "Who is to pay all this?"

The Emperor of Russia, going through the barracks to inspect the soldiers, passed this young man, who, with his head in his arms, had fallen asleep. The emperor, glancing at the figures before him on the table, read the question, and then bending over wrote one word, "Nicholas."

And the story goes that that one man was free. I do not know whether this story is true, but I do know that if you enumerate all of your sins from the earliest recollection to the present moment, and beneath the sum of them all write this question, "Who is to pay all this?" there will be one name written in answer to it,

"Sweetest name on mortal tongue,
Sweetest note in seraph song,
Sweetest carol ever sung,
Jesus, blessed Jesus."

## THEN FOLLOWS 'CONVERSION'

The third word starting from the letter "C" would be *"Conversion,"* and this we find in the Philippian jailor, for we are told, he "washed their stripes." This was surely a great change in the man. At first he exultingly fastened their feet in the stocks, and now I can imagine him tearfully stooping down with cooling touch to ease their pain. There must be conversion if we are ever to be saved.

I am speaking of the new birth, that is, God's part of it; but I am emphasizing the thing man must do if he is ever to see the light. In one way it is "Right about face!" or it is following the example of the blind men who "put themselves in the way of Jesus"; or it is the obedience of the lepers who, as they went, were cleansed. Indeed, to sum it all up, it is for the unsaved man to have "the willing mind." (Isaiah 1:19)

God never saved any man until, first of all, he was willing to be saved; so whether one kneels at the altar, or bows in prayer in his own home, or stands in the crowded audience, or signs the inquirer's card, the end of all these things must be the submission of the will to God; and then He does His own work, and we are born again, or from above.

## 'CONFESSING' CHRIST BEFORE MEN

The fourth and last word to be completed from the letter "C" is *"Confession,"* and this is clearly found in the experience of the jailor; for we are told he "was baptized." What a mistake it is for a man to believe in his heart and fail to confess with his lips! Such a position is never satisfactory, and never brings real joy. It is not being obedient, to say the least. If your physician should write a prescription for you in your sickness, and you should have it filled in a peculiar way, putting in two parts and leaving out two parts, he would have the right to find fault with you and tell you that you would never get well until you took the whole prescription. It is true with the Great Physician in our sin sickness; he has written the prescription that assures us of life. It is composed of two parts. (Romans 10:9,10):

First. Believe in your heart that Jesus is the Christ, the Son of God, and acknowledge Him as Lord.

Second. Confess with your lips that you have appropriated Him, not as a Saviour, but as your Saviour, for if one desires to be fully saved he must commit himself. It is not walking with the army that constitutes one a soldier; it is not the wearing of the garment of a soldier that makes him such, for this may be hired or stolen; but it is the definite enlistment, and this comes to one who would be a soldier of Jesus Christ when he definitely and clearly confesses Him. This is his enlistment.

## THE QUERY OF THE UNSAVED

"What, therefore, must I do to be saved?" This seems to be the unsaved man's first query. Philosophy has never yet answered this question. Infidelity has tried it, and made it a mockery. God's answer is clear and simple. The Bible says, "By grace are ye saved through faith; and that not of yourselves: it is the gift of God." "Not of works, lest any man should boast." It is very easy to receive a gift; the first step in salvation is not to give something, but rather to receive; then receiving eternal life, you may give yourself unto Him for service.

Man would naturally say, if you would be a son of God, try to walk as a son and you will eventually become such. But God makes it very clear that there can be no real life until there is a step taken, first of all, by faith; then He reveals Himself. The things of God are spiritually discerned, and God is a revelation, not an explanation. To make it very clear, the best answer is the one given to the Philippian jailor: "Believe on the Lord Jesus Christ, and thou shalt be saved." There is something very significant in the way the names of Jesus Christ are used. For example, when He is called Lord, it is to emphasize His kingly office, or His reigning power; and what can the meaning be but this, when we are told to believe on him as Lord? We must reach the place where we are willing to let Him rule and reign in our life. Can you submit to this? He will never make a failure of it. Give Him absolute control; never take a step without His guidance - this is the secret of grace and joy.

Jesus is the earthly name, and we are told that, "thou shalt call his name Jesus, for he shall save his people from their sins." It must be necessary, then, for one to get a conception of Him as He hangs upon the cross; and certainly we know He was there for just one purpose, namely, "that he might die in our stead."

Major Whittle tells the story of a company of bushwackers, arrested in Missouri during the days of the Civil War. They were sentenced to be shot, when a young boy touched the commanding officer on the arm and said, "Won't you allow me to take the place of the man standing yonder? He has a family, and he will be greatly missed; no one will miss me. May I take his place?" When the officer had given his consent, the young boy stepped forward, drew the man out of line and stepped in his place. When the command was given to fire, the boy fell dead; his grave is still to be found in the little Missouri town, and on the little stone that marks it are cut these words, "Sacred to the memory of Willie Lear; he took my place." The commanding officer's name was John McNeill, and the story was vouched for recently by one of the officer's personal friends in Evansville, Ind.

This is true of Jesus Christ; He died that we might live, but we must accept Him. There is no life except in Him, and the idea of substitution is found in all the Bible. He is also called Christ, but this is His resurrection name, and as Christ he stands this moment at the right hand of God, making intercession for us. Can you accept Him there?

It does seem to me that this makes the whole Christian life very plain. He is my Lord, because He rules me; He is Jesus, because He died to save me; and He is Christ because, whenever the mistakes of life overtake me, He stands at God's right hand to make explanation and intercession. Do you thus receive Him?

It is also to be remembered that, in the case of the Philippian jailor, light came in all its clearness when "they spake unto him the word of the Lord." I have very little confidence in that man who is not founded upon God's Word for assurance of his salvation. I have all the hope imaginable for that one who will receive it with meekness. I do not mean that he should be able at once to explain it; I only ask that by faith he receive it (John 5:24). I am persuaded that, if we could only persuade men to receive the Word of God, it would mean a joy unspeakable and a peace which the world cannot give, neither take away. One could not live in the promise and declaration of John's third chapter and sixteenth verse without rejoicing in hope. Say it over and over to yourself this way, and thus make it your own verse: "God so loved 'me' that he gave his only begotten Son that 'I' might believe in him and should not perish, but have everlasting life."

I would not have you forget in this interesting story of the jailor, that he was baptized. Baptism is inseparably connected with believing and is as certainly a command of God's as that we believe. We may differ as to the mode, but too much emphasis cannot be placed upon the command itself; it is, of course, true that one may be saved without it, as, for example, the thief on the cross; as for him, it was impossible; but I should be afraid to run the risk when Jesus said, "He that believeth and is baptized shall be saved, and he that believeth not shall be damned." At least, when we stand before Him, we could but say that we had neglected to do as He commanded. It is the experience of Christians everywhere that this one of the sacraments brings upon the believer a marvelous blessing, and leads him out into an experience, which can never be described in words.

It is not to be forgotten that when all these steps had been taken by the Philippian jailor he rejoiced, believing in God, with all his house. That word is certainly true that "in his presence is fullness of joy, and at his right hand there are pleasures for evermore." And why should it not be so?

One of my friends, a Scotsman, told me that some time ago he was going through his native land and stopped at a little cottage by the wayside to rest; when he entered the room his first inclination was to be seated in a very comfortable chair, which occupied a prominent place in the room; but just as he made the attempt an old Scotswoman sprang to the chair and, lifting her hand, exclaimed, "Nay, nay, man; don't sit there," and then she pointed to the scarlet cord fastened around the chair, which he had not noticed before, and explained, "One day Her Majesty, the Queen, a sudden storm coming upon her, left her carriage and came into this house." And, with a look of great reverence, this venerable woman added: "She sat in this chair, and when she went away we fastened this scarlet cord about it, and I said, "We will give it to John, and he can keep it in his family," for was it not wonderful that Her Majesty, the Queen, had used it?" But I have a greater cause for rejoicing; Jesus Christ, the King of kings has counted it a joy to take up His abode in my heart. He has cast around me the scarlet cord, which marks me as His own. It is a great thing for me to say that He is mine, but it is far greater for me to declare that I am His, and with the Philippian jailor, therefore, I rejoice with exceeding great joy.

# CLARENCE EDWARD NOBLE MACARTNEY

∞

C larence Edward Noble Macartney was born in 1879 in Northwood, Ohio. He graduated from the University of Wisconsin, Princeton University, and Princeton Theological Seminary. He was ordained to the ministry of the Presbyterian Church and his first pastorate was in First Church, Paterson, New Jersey. He then went on to serve in Arch Street Church, Philadelphia. In 1924 he was elected as moderator of the General Assembly of the Northern Presbyterian Church, USA in 1924 and for twenty-seven years he pastored the influential First Presbyterian Church of Pittsburgh Pennsylvania.

He was gifted in preaching Bible characters, and in this respect has been called 'the American Alexander White.' He was the author of more than forty publications, which included historical studies, sermons and biblical exegesis, among them *You Can Conquer; Prayer at the Golden Altar* and *The Greatest Questions of the Bible and Life* from which this sermon is taken.

# Chapter Three

# WHAT MUST I DO TO BE SAVED?

*And suddenly there was a great earthquake, so that the
foundations of the prison were shaken: and immediately all the
doors were opened, and every one's bands were loosed.
And the keeper of the prison awaking out of his sleep,
and seeing the prison doors open, he drew out his sword,
and would have killed himself,
supposing that the prisoners had been fled.
But Paul cried with a loud voice, saying,
Do thyself no harm: for we are all here.
Then he called for a light, and sprang in,
and came trembling, and fell down before Paul and Silas,
And brought them out, and said, Sirs, what must I do to be saved?*
- Acts 16:26-30

Good men who were prisoners sometimes conferred great benefits
on their jailors. We need but mention John Brown and John Bunyan
among others. But never did a prisoner confer so great a benefit on
his jailer as Paul did on the jailor of Philippi. When Jesus sent the
devils out of the man of Gadara into the swine, the owners of the

swine besought Jesus to depart out of their coasts. The fall in the pork market meant more to them than the redemption of a lost and devil-possessed man. This same spirit appeared at Philippi, when, because Paul had cast out the spirit of divination which possessed a poor girl there and thus deprived her masters of a profit, they brought false charges against Paul and Silas, that they were breaking the laws of Rome and stirring up sedition, and had them cast into prison. The magistrates did not take the time to make much of an investigation, never imagining that at least one of these strolling mendicant preachers was a Roman citizen, but had them stripped of their clothes and cruelly beaten. In the catalogue of his woes and sufferings, Paul afterwards wrote, "Thrice was I beaten with rods." This cruel outrage at Philippi was the first of those beatings. It was a barbarous and ferocious form of punishment under which the victim not infrequently succumbed, the kind of scourging to which Christ Himself was subjected by Pilate. Faint and bleeding from their wounds, Paul and Silas were cast into prison, into the innermost dungeon, a dark and foul den, where their hands and feet and necks were made fast in the stocks. Their situation was the last word in human misery and distress. How did they take it?

John in a dungeon lost his faith for a little and sent a message of doubt to Jesus. But here is no despair, no rebellion, and no doubt. At midnight Paul and Silas prayed and sang praises unto God, and the prisoners heard them. In their prayers they, must have remembered the magistrates who had condemned them, those in Philippi who had come to believe on Jesus, their fellow prisoners, and the jailor himself. I wonder what they were singing? I think one of the songs must have been Psalm 23: "Though I walk through the valley of the shadow of death, I will fear no evil: for thou art with me"; or perhaps Psalm 34: "I will bless the Lord at all times.... This poor man cried, and the Lord heard him, and saved him out of all his troubles"; or Psalm 46: "God is our refuge and strength, a very present help in trouble"; or Psalm 102: "For he hath looked down from the height of his sanctuary; from heaven did the Lord behold the earth; to hear the groaning of the prisoner; to loose those that are appointed to death." Paul knew well the promise of the Old Testament, "God ... giveth songs in the night." Now that promise was made real in his own life. It's a great hour for us when some verse of the Bible ceases to be rhetoric and becomes a blessed experience.

I have visited jails at midnight and there have heard strange music, the sob of remorse breaking from the breast of a first transgressor, the groan of despair, the appeal of the victim of narcotics, the shriek of the hysterical prostitute, and the malediction of the criminal. This was the kind of music, which hitherto had echoed within the walls of this old jail. But now they heard a different melody, and all the prisoners heard them singing. You can never tell where your voice will be heard or how far your influence will go, sometimes to the most unlikely places and persons. These prisoners heard them singing and at first answered with jest and ribald laughter. The child-stealer from Ephesus said, "What angels are these who have come to our palace?" The robber and bandit from the Egnatian highway said, "They can sing now, but by the morning, they will have learned our language and pitched their voices to our music." The murderer from Thessalonica said with an oath, "Would that this right arm of mine were free, and I would smash their teeth in with my fist and stop their singing." But still the apostles sang on, and at length a hush of silence and wonder fell over the dark and dismal dungeon. Tears stole down cheeks which long had been strangers to them. Thoughts of innocence and long forgotten happiness came back to these hardened criminals, and many a heart grew soft with recollections of yesterday, and from many a breast came a sigh which was dangerously near a prayer. The song of Paul and Silas had reached their hearts.

Down in the human heart, crushed by the tempter;
Feelings lie buried that grace can restore.

Perhaps when they were through singing, the bandit of the Egnatian Way asked them to sing it over again. Perhaps it was the first time, but certainly not the last, that men have made such a request.

Sing them over again to me,
Wonderful words of life.

Suddenly there was an earthquake, which shook the foundations of the prison, broke its doors, and loosed the chains from every prisoner. There was nothing strange about that. Philippi was in an earthquake zone, and the time and place were conspicuous for convulsions of this nature. When the jailor wakened out of his sleep and saw that the prison doors were open and took for granted that his prisoners had escaped, he drew his sword and was about to fall on it, following the example of other suicides in that vicinity, notably Brutus, who had fled not with their feet, but with their hands. A jail escape in that ancient day was a more serious thing than with us today, for then it meant that a jailor's life was forfeited.

But before the jailor could kill himself Paul cried out, "Do thyself no harm: for we are all here." What a fine description that is of the Gospel, which has for its mission to save men from the self-inflicted wound and bondage of sin. Amazed to discover that his prisoners had not fled, the jailor cried out, "What, must I do to be saved?" He was not asking how he could be saved from the earthquake, for its tremors had passed and he was safe. Neither was he asking how he could be saved from the wrath of Caesar for letting the prisoners escape, because the prisoners were all safe. No, it was from something else than the earthquake's shock and the judgment of Caesar that the jailor desired to be saved. In some way the conviction had been brought home to him that he was lost, and he wanted to know how to be saved. How did he come to have the idea of being saved? Perhaps, when impatiently trying to sleep, he had heard Paul and Silas pray for his salvation. Perhaps he had heard the demented maid who cried out, "These men are the servants of the most high God, which show unto us the way of salvation." But however he had come to the knowledge of it, this jailor knew that there was such a thing as salvation, and he wanted it. What shall I do? And still echoing down the ages comes the quick answer of the apostles, "Believe on the Lord Jesus Christ, and thou shalt be saved." This was followed up by Paul and Silas speaking unto him the Word of the Lord, and telling him the way of eternal life; that is, who Christ was, what He had done, and how He saved men. Then the jailor confessed his faith and, like the other converts in the New Testament, was baptized, for with the heart man believeth and with the mouth confession is made unto life.

## OTHER GREAT CONVERSIONS

This conversion was sudden and dramatic. It was accompanied by an earthquake. The converted man was full of excitement, emotion, and alarm. Some great men have been converted that way. One was Paul. Another was Luther, who, terrified by a thunderstorm as he was going through the wood to his home at Erfurt, fell on his knees and determined to give his life to God, which at that time meant entering a monastery. John Newton started toward God while the ship on which he was a passenger was being tossed in a storm on the wild Atlantic. Peter Waldo, generally thought to be the first of the Waldensians, was changed from a carefree man of the world to a servant of Christ when a friend who was seated near him at a banquet in Lyons fell dead, and Waldo asked himself, "Where would I now be if it had been I who had fallen dead?" One of the most eloquent of Presbyterian divines of the last century left college and entered the Civil War a skeptic, proud of his unbelief. But when in battle a cannon ball annihilated his companion, who was lying with him face down on the earth during an artillery bombardment, his unbelief and skepticism were blown up, and he entered the ministry. Some come into the Kingdom of God by the earthquake gate.

But others come in other ways. As if to make that clear, we have side by side here in the same chapter the story of the conversion of the first two converts of Europe, one this man who came to God with an earthquake, and the other Lydia, the purple seller, devout and prayerful, whose heart the Lord opened. She came as naturally and noiselessly as the coming of the morning. John Bunyan came by the earthquake route, the Slough-of-Despond path; but in his great common sense he was wise enough to know that not everyone had to travel his way - So he tells us of old Mr. Honest, living in the town of Stupidity, who, although that town was three degrees off the sun, was warmed by its rays and started for the Kingdom of Heaven.

There was no doubt about the genuineness of this conversion. It was so genuine that it embraced his whole house. His wife, his children, and his servants all followed the example of the jailor. "I hear my father pray at prayer meeting, but I never hear him pray at home," said a young man of his father. But the real thing will make a man pray, not only at prayer meeting, but in his own house. This conversion was one which brought forth fruit. What a picture that is, this jailer, in the best room of his own house, in the light of flickering torches, tenderly sponging with his own hands the bleeding backs of Paul and Silas, and then setting before them the best that his house had to offer, and they the very men whom he had thrust into the innermost dungeon and left without bread and water to their misery! A true conversion breaks up the hard places in a man's heart. It makes the cruel man a kind man, and the unjust man a just man.

The great question of the jailor and the great answer of the apostle is a splendid illustration of the way of salvation. Who is responsible for this word "save" and its corresponding word "lost"? Christ Himself. It was He who said, "The Son of man is come to seek and to *save* that which was *lost"*; and it was Christ Himself who was responsible for the answer which Paul gave to the jailor when he told him he could be saved by faith in Christ. There is no other way by which man can be saved. When Jesus, in that great scene of repentance and conversion before He had died on the cross, dismissed the woman who was a sinner, He said, "Thy faith hath saved thee; go in peace."

Just what faith is, and how it saves a man, Paul made clear in his midnight sermon to the alarmed jailor. He did not stop with telling him merely, "Believe, and thou shalt be saved." He explained to him, we may be sure, for he spoke to him the word of the Lord, who Christ is, and what He has done for the sinner. Faith ultimately and finally means faith in Christ's saving work on the cross. To believe in Christ is to believe in Him as the Savior from sin. Until you take Christ in that way and in that great sense, you have never really received Him. You may believe in Him as God's Son, or as a great and even divine Friend, Teacher, and Companion; but you have not really believed on Him until you believe on Him as your Savior.

## WE ARE SAVED BY FAITH

That faith is the only way to be saved is clearly shown when we take the great passages of Scriptures dealing with this subject, and where the word "believe" is used, substitute for it its Greek equivalent "have faith." The verb "believe" always comes from the noun "faith." Take these passages as examples, where we substitute "have faith" for "believe": "God so loved the world, that he gave his only begotten Son, that whosoever *hath faith in* him should not perish, but have everlasting life." "Verily, verily, I say unto you, He that *hath faith* on me hath everlasting life." "Go ye into all the world, and preach the gospel to every creature. He that *hath faith* and is baptized shall be saved. "What must I do to be saved? ... *Have faith* on the Lord Jesus Christ, and thou shalt be saved." The offer of salvation is free; the gate to heaven is as wide as the mercy of God. But this free salvation is not unconditional. It has one, only one, but nevertheless one condition - the sinner's faith in Christ.

Since we are saved by faith, we know that our own character and our own good works have nothing to do with it. If Paul had told this jailor he could be saved by his past record, it would have been a message of despair, for he had no good works to which be could point. In the second place, such a way of salvation by faith in Christ signally honors the Son of God. God chooses not only to save man, but to save him in a way which shall glorify His Son. In the third place, this way of salvation is for us a free way and an easy way. Christ did the hard part. His were the tears, the groans, the sighs, the agony, the cross, and the awful darkness. It is because the way was so hard for Christ that it is so easy for you. Indeed, so easy that some miss it altogether.

What a Christ we have in whom to have faith! To whom shall we go but unto Him? Do you believe? Then prove it, as this jailor did by his acts of mercy and kindness and the joy of his heart. If you have not believed, will you not now believe? Why wait for that and for Him who is waiting for you? Do not question the truth of it. Do not be kept back by a lack of feeling or the lack of a good record or a lack of what you think is fit repentance. What Christ said, what Paul said to the jailor, was not *to feel* this way or that way, *do* this or that, lay claim to this or that good act in the past, but *believe,* have faith in the Lord Jesus Christ, and thou shalt be saved. We cannot measure all that "have faith" means. But neither can we measure all that "thou shalt be saved" means. Perhaps, indeed, the jailor by this time could tell you and me something about it. But all that it does mean, for that we shall have to wait until we stand by the jailor's side before the throne of the Lamb and sing our praise unto Him who came to seek and to save that which was lost.

# HYMAN J. APPLEMAN

⚭

D
r. Hyman J. Appleman was born in Russia and raised in the Jewish faith. His family immigrated to America in 1914 and he graduated with honours from North Western University and DePaul University. He received his license to practice law from DePaul Law School and became a highly successful trial lawyer in Chicago. After his conversion to Christ when he was 28 years of age, his family disowned him but, assured that the Lord was calling him to preach, he studied at South Western Baptist Theological Seminary in Fort Worth. In 1933 he was appointed to be one of the State Evangelists for Texas. After eight years in this ministry he started to receive invitations to preach at various meetings and conventions in many countries and such was the power of his preaching that many thousands of souls were led to Christ through his ministry. Dr. Appleman made nine trips around the world including his native Russia and he was also the author of over forty books, including the volume *The Saviour's Invitation* from which this sermon 'Saved' is taken.

Chapter Four

# SAVED

☙

*And at midnight Paul and Silas prayed,*
*and sang praises unto God: and the prisoners heard them.*
*And suddenly there was a great earthquake, so that the*
*foundations of the prison were shaken: and immediately all the*
*doors were opened, and every one's bands were loosed. And the*
*keeper of the prison awaking out of his sleep, and seeing the*
*prison doors open, he drew out his sword, and would have killed*
*himself, supposing that the prisoners had been fled.*
*But Paul cried with a loud voice, saying, Do thyself no harm: for*
*we are all here. Then he called for a light, and sprang in,*
*and came trembling, and fell down before Paul and Silas,*
*And brought them out, and said,*
*Sirs, what must I do to be saved?*
*And they said, Believe on the Lord Jesus Christ,*
*and thou shalt be saved, and thy house.*
*And they spake unto him the word of the Lord,*
*and to all that were in his house.*
*And he took them the same hour of the night, and washed their*
*stripes; and was baptized, he and all his, straightway.*
*And when he had brought them into his house, he set meat before*
*them, and rejoiced, believing in God with all his house.*
*- Acts 16:25-34*

☙

May this meditation help you to consider seriously the vital question *What must I do to be saved?* It is the most important question in all the Bible, in all the world. Problems beset us on every hand, but this is the most important of all. If you solve any other problem incorrectly you may suffer for it, but the consequences will not be eternal. However, this problem involves both time and eternity. Other decisions may be local, individual, but this query is universal.

This is a personal question. We cannot decide it for each other. We are not born in crowds. We do not die in crowds. We are not saved in crowds. We are not lost in crowds. One by one we must face Calvary, the death angel, the judgment, eternity.

This is a pressing question. There is no escaping it. There is no denying it. There is no hiding from it. There is no being indifferent to it. We must face it because it will not let us escape from its implications. When it ceases to trouble us it is only because we have already accepted Jesus Christ as our Saviour, or have fallen so far into sin that the Spirit of God has stopped striving with us.

Because of the importance of this great thought, it behooves us to learn all we can of it, to study it thoroughly, to analyze it, to come to a definite decision regarding it. Let us, therefore, approach the question from three angles.

First, why should we be saved?
Second, what must we do to be saved?
Third, when shall we be saved?

We should be saved, first, because of the value of our souls. In substance, each of us has a body, a mind, a soul. These three are all important, but the soul is by far the most important. There are many ways in which we can take care of our bodies. We can eat the right kind of food, take the proper exercise, sleep the required number of hours, spend time in the fresh air. Occasionally we need medicine. Sometimes a surgical operation is required. There are many ways in which we can provide for our bodies.

There are also many methods which we can employ in the training and care of the mind. We can go to school. We can study, read, meditate, listen to others, practice, exercise. It is perfectly proper, fully essential to see that our bodies and minds have the best of sustenance. But what about the soul? There is but one way to take care of the soul: by salvation. Nothing can touch the soul but the regenerating power of God's Holy Spirit.

One of these days our bodies will die. They will molder in some cemetery. Our minds will disintegrate with our bodies. But our souls will go on forever with God in heaven or the Devil in hell.

We should be saved, second, because of the difference between heaven and hell. Think of heaven's characteristics. It is a realm of life, of love, of light, of laughter. There is no sickness there, no sorrow, no suffering. There are no disappointments there, no disturbances, no discouragements. Wars are unknown. Want is vanquished. Woe is outlawed. The afflictions of the flesh do not prevail. It is the delightsome land of our fondest dreams, our loftiest imaginings.

Think of the company in heaven. God is there, and Christ, and the Holy Spirit. All the children who died in their infancy are there, rosebuds transplanted into the garden of God. The gentlest, the finest, the sweetest, the purest of the earth, those washed in the blood of the Lamb are there, forever serving God in His holy temple.

Think of what characterizes hell. It is a place of darkness, of torment, of eternal banishment from God, of pain, of anguish, of weeping, or unavailing remorse. Think of the company in hell. The vilest, the filthiest, the most corrupt, the most wicked in all creation are the denizens of the pit. People with whom you would shudder to associate compose hell's crowd. On earth you can choose your associates. In hell you are forever cast into the society of that awful bedlam, never to find release or relief from their lewdness, their corruption, their frightfulness. Yes, the difference between heaven and hell should lead you to seek salvation.

The third reason why we ought to be saved is this: the endlessness of eternity. If you could go to hell for a million years and then go to heaven, you would at last have deliverance. A million years would eventually pass. But heaven and hell are *forever.* The minute you accept Christ as your personal Saviour you start on the journey to heaven, never to finish until you stand complete, glorified in Christ before God, and establish your abode in the mansions of bliss forever and ever.  If you reject Christ, there is nothing you can do in time or eternity that will keep or take you from the torment of hell or release you from it.  *And the smoke of their torment ascendeth up forever and ever: and they have no rest day nor night.*  That is a frightful thought that should make all of us pause, that should constrain all of us to flee from the wrath to come.  There is no way out of heaven. There is no way out of hell.

The fourth reason why we ought to be saved is perhaps not so self-centered and yet it is also eminently personal.  It is because of our influence upon others.  There is not one of you who would willingly, knowingly, consciously cause anybody to stumble over your unbelief into destruction.  There is not one of you who would not gladly do anything, everything to keep a soul out of hell and start it on the road to heaven.  You may if you wish.  If you give your own heart to the Lord Jesus Christ, surrender your own life to Him in service, God will use you.  God will bless and empower your testimony.  I do not care how weak, how small you think yourself to be, God can and will use you to win others to the Lord Jesus Christ.

For these four reasons –

the value of your soul,

the difference between heaven and hell,

the endlessness of eternity,

your influence upon others

- every one of you ought to accept Jesus Christ as Saviour in this very hour, then go out to live a consistent, consecrated, fruit-bearing life, a truly Christian life.

What must we do to be saved?  If I told you out of my own heart or mind, if I gave you my own theological answer, you would have a right to hesitate, to question, to doubt.  But I will let God tell you what you must do.  There are three conditions essential for salvation. Regardless of what anyone may say, the Bible is the Rule Book. There are three things - not one, not two, but *three* - with which you must comply ere you may consider yourself free from all sin.

First, you must *repent.*  *Seek ye the Lord while he may be found, call ye upon him while he is near: let the wicked forsake his way, and the unrighteous man his thoughts: and let him return unto the Lord, and he will have mercy upon him; and to our God, for he will abundantly pardon* (Isaiah 55:6-7). That is perhaps the Bible's clearest statement of this first requisite. You must turn your backs on your sins, on yourselves, on each other. You must turn your faces to God. In substance you must plead, "Lord, I know I am a sinner. I know I cannot save myself. I know Jesus Christ died for my sins. I know He can save me. Lord, have mercy on me a sinner."

The second step all of you know. The greatest statement of it is found in John 3:16: *For God so loved the world, that he gave his only begotten Son, that whosoever believeth in him should not perish, but have everlasting life.* You must believe in the Lord Jesus Christ. What does it mean to believe in Him? You must believe that He is the Son of God, that He died for your sins, that God raised Him from the dead, that He is sitting at the right hand of God, interceding for all of us, that He can save you, that He wants to save you, that He will save you if you trust Him.

There is one more thing you must do to be saved. You will find it mentioned in the Bible at least twice: once from the lips of Jesus and once from the pen of Paul. Jesus said, *Whosoever therefore shall confess me before men, him will I confess also before my Father which is in heaven.* Paul wrote, *That if thou shalt confess with thy mouth, the Lord Jesus, and shalt believe in thine heart that God hath raised him from the dead, thou shalt be saved. For with the heart man believeth unto righteousness; and with the mouth confession is made unto salvation* (Romans 10:9-10). You must confess Christ as your personal Saviour.

Our last question is: *When should we be saved?* Yesterday is gone. Some of you, perhaps, many of you, should have been saved yesterday, but yesterday is gone. It is too late to talk about it now. Not even God can call back those yesterdays. Shall you wait until tomorrow? How do you know you will be alive tomorrow? Will you want salvation more tomorrow than you do today? You know that every day of delay makes it just so much harder. Every day you postpone it you will want salvation less than the day before. How do you know God will want to save you tomorrow? Perhaps you say, "God will want to save me any time." That is not what my Bible says. It declares, *He, that being often reproved hardeneth his neck, shall suddenly be destroyed, and that without remedy ... My spirit shall not always strive with man.* You dare not take a chance with God.

One night when I was conducting a revival, a boy came down the aisle, accepted Christ as his Saviour, and offered himself for baptism. The following Saturday night, a little before church time, he walked into his mother's room and spoke to her. "Mother, I have a terrible headache. I'm going to take my motorcycle and drive around awhile, and then go on to church." He used that motorcycle every day, and his mother saw no cause for concern. That night when I arrived home from church I received a call to "come quickly." Two motorcycle policemen cruising down the northwest highway had found the crushed motorcycle on one side of the road and the body of the boy on the other. He was dead. The following Tuesday his funeral was held. I attended. The church was crowded with people. Flowers were everywhere. There was barely room for the minister to stand in the pulpit. When the pastor told the story of the boy's stand for Christ, his friends thanked God for his conversion. His father and mother thanked God through their bitter tears that their son was saved. Supposing that boy had said, "Tomorrow." His soul would have gone down into hell - everlasting hell.

There is only one time to be saved and that is today. There is only one time to repent and that is today. There is only one time to take a public stand for Christ and that is today. There is only one time today and that is *now.* There is only one time now and that is this hour. There is only one time this hour and that is this minute. Accept Christ as your personal Saviour now. Accept the offer of His matchless mercy now. Heed the call of the Spirit *now.* Say "yes" to God now. Step out on the Lord's invitation and promises now.

Dr. George Truett tells the following story again and again. He held a service in his own junior Department in his own great church. He gave the invitation. Seventy juniors came down the aisles for the Lord Jesus Christ. Most of them joined the church. Dr. Truett went about his business. That Thursday he received a telephone call from the Baylor Hospital in Dallas. A sick girl wanted to see him. The little girl, Nellie by name, was ill with influenza. Her father and mother were with her, and Doctor Truett led them in prayer.

When he started for the door, the little girl - one of those who had accepted Christ on the previous Sunday - called him back.

"Will you do me a favor?" she asked.

"Certainly. What is it?"

"Will you go to my department Sunday and ask for me? If I am not there tell them where I am, and ask them to pray for me. Tell them Nellie said she wasn't afraid, because she has trusted Christ."

Sunday Dr. Truett saw that the child was not in Sunday school. He delivered her message and went on about his preaching. Saturday another telephone call came. Nellie was dying. Her parents wanted to see Dr. Truett. He rushed to the hospital, and found the mother and father standing at the foot of their little girl's bed, weeping. The child was stretched out on her back. Her eyes were closed, and her face was pale with approaching death. Dr. Truett talked quietly to her parents. After awhile the girl, opening her eyes, saw her mother and father weeping. Moistening her dry lips, in a hoarse, small voice, she asked, "Why are you crying?"

They cried all the harder, naturally. Dr. Truett answered,

"Because you are going to leave them. You are going to be with Jesus." It took her awhile to understand. In a minute she understood.

"You mean I am going to die?" she asked.

"I'm sorry, but you are. You are leaving Daddy and Mamma and going to heaven."

She closed her eyes and whimpered softly, too ill to cry hard. Then she thought of something. Her face glowed with smiles. Lifting herself on her elbows in her eagerness, she said,

"I'm not afraid. I am a Christian. I am going to heaven. Don't cry, Daddy. Don't cry, Mamma. The first thing I am going to tell Jesus is how you both told me about Him, and got me to love Him. I will be waiting for you. Don't cry. Please don't cry."

She continued to comfort her mother and father. The minutes ticked along. Her face grew more pale. She turned to Dr. Truett. He got down on his knees and pressed his ear against her lips. She was whispering.

"Will you go to my department again Sunday? I won't be there, will I?"

"No. You will be in the Sunday school where Jesus is Superintendent, and the angels are the teachers."

"Will you tell them where I am? Tell them I was not afraid to die because I have trusted Christ. Tell them Nellie said for all of them to give their hearts to Jesus, so when they die they will not be afraid either."

That is Nellie's message to you. Oh, let it come into your hearts. Let it fill your minds. Let it thrill your souls. Let it move your wills. You must be saved. God wants to save you. Jesus Christ died to save you. The Holy Spirit invites you to be saved. In this hour, this moment, right now, turn from your sins, put your faith in the Lord Jesus Christ, accept Him and confess Him as your personal Saviour. God for Christ's sake will do the rest. You will then be a child of God, and you will be saved eternally.

# REUBEN ARCHER TORREY

∽

R euben Archer Torrey grew up in a wealthy home, and was educated at Yale University and Divinity School. It was while he was studying at Yale that his life took a downward turn and he became an agnostic and also a heavy drinker. But looking back on those days he would say that he had a conviction in his heart that some day he was going to be a preacher of the Gospel, and indeed the Lord did save him while he was in his senior year in college. When at Yale Divinity School he was largely influenced by D. L. Moody, who had come to town for a Gospel Campaign. Recognising his outstanding scholastic abilities and his evangelistic zeal, Moody later hand picked him to become superintendent of Moody Bible Institute, and soon he became his right hand man. He was pastor of Moody Church from 1894-1906, and in 1912 he became dean of BIOLA, where he served until 1924. After Moody's death he left the Bible Institute to carry on the great soul winning campaigns of the Moody pattern in Australia, New Zealand, England and America. When he died in 1928 he had written more than forty books. This sermon is taken from his book *"Revival Addresses."*

# Chapter Five

# THE WAY OF SALVATION
# MADE AS PLAIN AS DAY

☙

*Then he called for a light, and sprang in and came trembling,*
*and fell down, before Paul and Silas,*
*And brought them out, and said, Sirs, what must I do to be saved?*
*And they said, Believe on the Lord Jesus Christ,*
*and thou shalt be saved, and thy house.*
- Acts 16:29-31

☙

The Philippian jailor, by a train of circumstances, which I have read in the Scripture lesson tonight, had been brought to a realisation of the fact that he was a lost sinner, and had a deep yearning for salvation, and he put to Paul and Silas this direct question, "What must I do to be saved?" Paul answered him in the words of the text, "Believe on the Lord Jesus Christ and thou shalt be saved." Nothing could be plainer, nothing could be more direct, nothing could be more positive than that. The way of salvation is to believe on the Lord Jesus Christ, and the moment any man or woman *or child really believes on the Lord Jesus Christ, they are saved.* If the most utterly lost man or woman in London should come into this hall tonight, and should here, or in the after meeting, or after they have gone out, believe on the Lord Jesus, the moment they did it they would be saved. Someone may say, "But this was a word simply spoken to one man; what right have you to say that any man will be saved the same way?" Because the same thing is said over and over again in the Bible. For instance, you read in Acts 10:43: "To Him give all the prophets witness that through His name, *whosoever* believeth in Him shall receive remission of sins." There isn't a man or woman in this building tonight that needs to go out of it without all their sins being forgiven and blotted out. It is just one act, "Believe on the Lord Jesus and thou shalt be saved."

## 1. WHAT IT MEANS TO BELIEVE ON THE LORD JESUS

What does it mean to believe on the Lord Jesus? We need to be very careful in our answer to that question, for there are many answers to it that are inaccurate and untrue. There are men who say and think that they believe on the Lord Jesus, and yet they do not. What does it mean to believe on the Lord Jesus? I have given a very careful and thorough study to this subject; I have gone all through my Bible looking, up the word " believe," and all words related to it, and I have found out what I suspected to be the fact when I began, viz., that "believe" means in the Bible just exactly what it means in modern speech. What is it to believe on a man? To believe on a man means to put confidence in him as what he claims to be. To believe on a physician means to put confidence in him as a physician, resulting in your placing your case in his hands. To believe in a teacher is to put your confidence in him as a teacher, and accept what he teaches; to believe in a banker means to put your confidence in him as a banker, and to put your money in his bank. And to believe on the Lord Jesus means to put your confidence in Him as what He claims to be.

To put confidence in the Lord Jesus as what? As all that He claims to be, and all that He offers Himself to be. What does the Lord Jesus claim to be, and what does He offer Himself to be?

1.   In the first place, the Lord Jesus offers Himself to every one of us as a *Sin-bearer.* In Matthew 20:28 He says, "The Son of Man came not to be ministered unto, but to minister, and *to give His life a ransom for* many." He offers Himself as a ransom for all. That thought runs all through the Bible, in the Old Testament as well as in the New. If you want to find it in the Old Testament, turn to Isaiah 53:6: "All we like sheep have gone astray; we have turned every one to his own way; and the Lord hath laid on Him (that is, on the Lord Jesus) the iniquity of us all." If you want to find it in the New Testament turn to 1 Peter 2:24: "Who His own self bare our sins in His own body on the tree, that we, being dead to sins, should live unto righteousness: by whose stripes ye were healed." Christ offers Himself to every man as a Sin-bearer, and to believe on the Lord Jesus is to put confidence in Him as your Sin-bearer.

2.   In the second place, the Lord Jesus offers Himself to us as a *Deliverer from the power of sin.* He says in John 8:34, "Whosoever committeth sin is the servant of sin." And we all know that is true; for we have all committed sin, and become the bond-servants of sin, and no man is able to break away from sin in his own strength. He says, in John 8:36, "If the Son therefore shall make you free, ye shall be free indeed." The Lord Jesus offers Himself to each one of us as One who has power to set us free from the power of sin. He says that Satan is the strong man armed, but that Himself is stronger than Satan. To believe on the Lord Jesus is to put confidence in Jesus as One who has power to set you free from sin.

3.   In the third place, Christ offers Himself to us as a *divinely taught and absolutely infallible Teacher.* In John 14:10-11 He says, "The words that I speak unto you I speak not of Myself: but the Father that dwelleth in Me, He doeth the works. Believe Me that I am in the Father, and the Father in me: or else believe me for the very works' sake." He offers Himself to you as the Teacher who speaks to you the words of God, who speaks no words of His own; as the Teacher who dwells

in God, and in whom God dwells, a divinely taught and absolutely infallible Teacher; and to believe on Christ is to put confidence in Him as such.

4.    In the fourth place, the Lord Jesus offers Himself to us as *our Master, who has the right to the entire control of our lives.* In John 15:14 He says, "Ye are My friends if ye do whatsoever I command you." To believe on the Lord Jesus is to put confidence in Jesus as a Master who has the right to have the entire and absolute control of your life.

5.    Again, the Lord Jesus Christ offers Himself to us as *a light and guide.* He says in John 8:12, " I am the Light of the world; he that followeth Me shall not walk in darkness, but shall have the light of life." To believe on Jesus is to put confidence in Him as the Light of the world, as the One to follow wherever He leads.

6.    And lastly, the Lord Jesus offers himself to us as our Divine *Lord.* He says in John 13:13 "Ye call me Master and Lord: and ye say well; for so I am." And we read in John 20:28-29, that when Thomas saw Jesus Christ after His resurrection, and was convinced at last that He really was raised from the dead, he threw up his hands and said to Jesus, "My Lord and my God!" And Jesus commended Thomas for this confession, saying to him, "Thomas, because thou hast seen Me, thou hast believed: blessed are they that have not seen, and yet have believed." Jesus offers Himself to us as our divine Lord. To believe on Jesus is to put confidence in Him as our divine Lord.

So, to sum it all up, to believe on the Lord Jesus Christ is to put confidence in Him as your Sin-bearer, as your Deliverer from the power of sin, as your divinely taught and absolutely infallible Teacher, as your Master who has the right to the entire control of your life, as your Light and Guide whom you will follow wherever He leads, and as your divine Lord. The moment you thus put your confidence, your absolute confidence in Jesus Christ, that moment you are saved. "Believe on the Lord Jesus Christ and thou shalt be saved."

## II.  HOW FAITH MANIFESTS ITSELF

But how will we show our faith?  In other words, if we really have believed on the Lord Jesus Christ and really have been saved, how will we show it?

1.　　In the first place, we will show it by *an assur*ance *that our, sins are all forgiven.*  If I really put my trust in Jesus as my Sin-bearer, put my trust in Him as One who has borne all my sin, past, present, and future, the moment I put confidence in Him as that, I know I don't bear them any longer, and I have assurance that every sin I have ever committed is forgiven. In Luke 7, we read of a woman who was a sinner.  She was an outcast.  But she came into a house where Jesus was reclining at the table, and men thought Jesus could be no prophet because He allowed her to touch Him.  But Jesus, when He saw her faith, said, "Thy sins are forgiven. Thy faith hath saved thee; go in peace."  When that woman went out of that place she knew that her sins were forgiven.  If you had met her on the street and had said, "Do you know your sins are forgiven?" she would have said "Yes, I know it; I am sure of it." "Why are you sure?" "Because He told me so, and I therefore know it."  "But do you feel it do you feel as if your sins were forgiven?"  Very likely she would reply, "I don't feel it yet; the news is so good I cannot realise it, but I am sure it is so; I know it, for He said so." "Well," you might have said, "you must not be so sure unless you feel it." And she would have replied, "Oh, I am sure." But you will say, "How can you be sure if you don't feel it?" And she would say, "Because He said so."

2.　　Secondly, if you have believed on the Lord Jesus Christ, it will show itself *in your looking to Him and trusting in Him for victory over sin.*  If you put confidence in Him as the

Deliverer from the power of sin, you will certainly look to Him, and trust Him to set you free from the power of sin. You will not say, "My sins are so great that He cannot deliver me." You will not look at the greatness of your sin at all. You will look at the greatness of your Saviour.

A man came to me one day in Chicago, and said, "Mr. Torrey, I want to speak to you alone"; so I took him up to Mr. Moody's office - Mr. Moody was away at the time. He said, "I want to tell you my story." So I said "Very well; sit down"; and he began to tell me his life-story. He said: "Away over in Scotland, when I was but seven years of age, I started to read the Bible through" (a good thing for a boy to do) "and I got as far as Deuteronomy. Reading there I found that if a man kept the whole law for a hundred years, and then broke the law at any point, he was under a curse. Is that right?" I said, "Well, that is not an exact quotation, but it is about the substance of it." He continued, "I was only a boy of seven, but I was overwhelmed with the sense that I was under the curse of God, and that lasted for nearly a year. Then I got to the New Testament, and I read John 3:16: "God so loved the world, that He gave His only begotten Son, that whosoever believeth in Him should not perish but have everlasting life." Then I saw that the Lord Jesus had borne all my sin, and my burden rolled away." He said, "Was I converted?" I replied, "That sounds like an evangelical conversion." Then he said, "Wait a moment: let me tell the rest of my story. After some years I came to Chicago, and I am now working down in the stockyards. You know the stockyards neighbourhood: it is a very hard neighbourhood. I have got into drinking habits, and every little while I fall under the power of strong drink. I try to break away, but I cannot. What I have come to ask you is this, is there any way to get victory over sin?" I said, "You have come just to the right man; I can tell you that." "I wish you would," he said. I opened my Bible at 1 Corinthians 15, and I read the first four verses: "Moreover, brethren, I declare unto you the Gospel which I preached unto you, which also ye have received, and wherein ye stand; By which also ye are saved, if ye keep in memory what I preached unto you, unless ye have believed in vain. For I delivered unto you first of all that which I also received, how that *Christ died for our sins* according to the Scriptures; and that He was buried, and that *He rose* again the third day according to the Scriptures." "Now," I said, "you believed that Jesus Christ died for your sins." He said, "I did." "You found peace in believing." "I did." I said, "But you only believed half the Gospel, that Christ died for our sins according to the Scriptures, and was buried. Will you now believe the other half of the Gospel? Will you believe that *He, rose aqain?*" He said, "I do believe; I believe everything that is in the Bible." I said again, "Do you really believe that Jesus rose again?" and he said, "I do." I said, "Do you believe what Jesus Christ says in Matthew 28:18, "All power is given unto Me in heaven and in earth." "Yes." "Then He has got power to set you free from the power of sin. Do you believe it?" He said, "I do." I said, "Will you put your trust in Him right now, to do it?" He said, "I will." "All right," I said, "let us kneel down," and then I prayed, and he followed with a prayer something like this: "Oh God, I believed that Jesus died for my sins on the Cross, and I found peace through believing, and now I believe that Jesus rose again, and that He has all power in Heaven and on earth, and He has got power to set me free today. Lord Jesus, set me free from the power of drink and the power of sin." When he had prayed, I said to him, "Will you trust Him to do it?" He said, "I will," and he did. In a few weeks I received a letter from that man in which he said, "I am so glad I came over to see you. *"It works!"*

Christ not only died, but He rose again, and is a living Saviour tonight. He has all power in heaven and in earth, and the devil is no match for Him; the risen Christ has power to snap the fetters of strong drink, to snap the fetters of opium, to snap the fetters of lust, and of every sin; and if you will trust Him to do it for you, He will do it. To believe on the Lord Jesus Christ means to look to Him and trust Him to give you victory over sin.

3.    In the third place, it will show itself in your *unquestioning acceptance of the infallible and absolute truth and authority of everything Jesus says.* – If I put confidence in Jesus as a divinely taught and absolutely infallible Teacher, whatever I find in the Bible that Jesus says, I will believe it. I may not understand it, it may seem impossible, and the scholars may be against me, but I believe in the Lord Jesus, and what He says I accept absolutely in all its height, depth, length, and breadth. Many people today claim to believe in the Lord Jesus, but if they find Jesus teaching one thing, and men tell them that the consensus of the latest scholarship teaches something else, they accept the consensus of the latest scholarship, and throw overboard the teaching of Christ. Gentlemen, I affirm that those men do not believe in the Lord Jesus. They believe in "the consensus of the latest scholarship," and believing in the consensus of the latest scholarship never saved any one. It has ruined many. How can you say you believe in Jesus if you don't believe Him? Belief in the Lord Jesus means to put confidence in Him, to put absolute confidence in Him as what He claims to be; and He claims to be a divinely taught Teacher that speaks only the words of God.

It is a critical time in which we live, and the question is, shall we believe German scholarship so called, or the Lord Jesus Christ? Well, in answer to that question, I say, the Lord Jesus Christ has stood for nineteen centuries, and German scholarship never stands for fifteen years consecutively; and I prefer to believe the Lord Jesus.

4.    Our belief in Him will be shown by *studying His Word.* If I believe in the Lord Jesus, I shall study His word over and over again. Suppose some man should come to London claiming to be a divinely taught and absolutely infallible teacher, and that you believed in him. Would you not read every word that he uttered? We have a man in America who claims not only to be a divinely taught and absolutely infallible teacher, but a messenger sent direct from God. Suppose I

believed he really was a teacher sent from God, I would study every word he said, as hundreds do in Chicago. They spend more time reading his words than they do reading their Bibles. Just so, if I believe in Jesus as what He claims to be, a divinely taught and absolutely infallible Teacher, what I shall study above all else will be the words of Jesus Himself.

5.  Faith in the Lord Jesus Christ will show itself by *a surrender of the entire life to His Control*. If I put confidence in Jesus as what He claims to be my Lord, having right to the absolute control of my life I will put my whole life in His control. Have you done it? You say you are a Christian, you believe in the Lord Jesus Christ. Are you proving it by putting your entire life in His control?

6.  In the next place, you will show your belief in the Lord Jesus Christ by *obedience to* Him in *daily life, in whatever He tells you to* do. In Luke 6:46 He says, "Why call ye Me Lord, Lord, and do not the things which I say?" I believe He is saying the same thing to the Christians of London, the professing christians. You call Him "Lord, Lord," every Sabbath day in your lives, and then you go through every day of the week living just as He tells you not to live, and you refuse to do what He plainly tells you to do. Now when the Lord Jesus was here on earth and healed men, He demanded faith as a condition precedent to healing, and He demanded that they should show their faith by their acts. He demands faith today as a condition precedent to salvation, and, having been saved, He demands that you show your faith by your acts, that you do what He tells you. That makes some of you look very uncomfortable. I am glad of it; it is a good sign. Some of you professed Christians need to be brought under conviction of sin. You have been praying that outsiders may be convicted of sin, but a whole lot of you need to be convicted of sin yourselves; and when you get convicted of sin more of the outsiders will be convicted of sin.

7.    Faith on the Lord Jesus Christ will show itself again in *following Him wherever He leads.* If I put confidence in Jesus Christ as the Light of the World, I will follow Him that I may "not walk in darkness, but have the Light of Life." "He that saith he abideth in Him ought himself so to walk *even as He walked."* Are you following in His steps, in your business, in your social life, in your personal life, in your individual life everywhere?

8.    Belief on the Lord Jesus Christ will show itself in *confessing Him before the world,* and *in witnessing for Him to men.* We read in Romans 10:9-10: "If thou shalt confess with thy mouth the Lord Jesus, and shalt believe in thine heart that God hath raised Him from the dead, thou shalt be saved. For with the heart man believeth unto righteousness; and with the mouth confession is made unto salvation."

I received a letter today from a man who said it was a very hard thing to expect people to stand up to confess Christ in the way I ask them to, and he went on to tell me an easier way to get at it. But I am not looking for an easier way. I abominate these easy ways. I believe in getting people converted. I could pass round cards and get them to sign their names, saying that they hoped to go to heaven; but a month after I had gone the effect would be nothing, or worse than nothing. I do not take any stock in any faith that does not lead to an open confession of Christ before the world, and I do not take any stock in the Christianity of your professed Christians unless it leads you to go out into the world and witness for the One who saved you. "Out of the abundance of the heart the mouth speaketh."

Now I put to you a question. Do you believe on the Lord Jesus Christ? You thought you did when you came in, but do you? I asked God in my prayer that He would sweep away false hopes tonight. Do you believe on the Lord Jesus Christ? It is one thing to say you believe, and another thing to believe. If you do not, will you believe on Him now, this moment? Will you put confidence in Jesus Christ this moment as your Sin-bearer, as a Deliverer from the power of sin, as a divinely taught and absolutely infallible Teacher, as the Lord who has the right to the absolute control of your life, as the Light of the World, as your Divine Lord? Will you do it? It takes but one instant to believe on the Lord Jesus Christ. It can be done in a moment. But it will take a whole lifetime to show that you have believed on Him after you have done it. The act of faith is instantaneous, the fruits of faith are life-long. Will you put your trust in Him tonight? If you do, the results will follow, and if you never did it before, you can do it now.

And you men and women who never professed to believe in the Lord Jesus Christ, will you put your confidence in the Lord Jesus Christ now? The moment you do it, you will be saved. I will tell any man or woman who is utterly unsaved, that in the next moment you may be saved. I will tell any man or woman who is utterly unsaved, who wishes to flee from underneath the wrath of God and come underneath the full sunlight of God's favour, that you can do it in an instant. How? Believe on the Lord Jesus Christ; put confidence in the Lord Jesus Christ as what He claims to be. If the vilest outcast in London should be in this room now and should here and now put confidence in Jesus as all He claims to be, the moment he did it God would blot out all his sin, and set to his account all the righteousness of Christ; and set him free from the power of sin, and transform him into a child of God. Old things in a moment would pass away and all things would become new. Oh the miracle of regeneration! I have seen a man one moment a drunkard, half drunk at the time, get his eyes open enough to see the truth about the Lord Jesus and put his trust in Him, and the next moment I was looking into the eyes of a child of God.

One night in Chicago, in the Pacific Garden Mission, there came in a poor fellow, a complete physical and moral wreck. He had been in a railroad accident, and was a total cripple, helpless on both feet, dragging himself along on crutches. For fourteen years he had been a victim of whisky and alcohol in all its forms, and of opium as well. He was an opium fiend and an alcohol fiend. My friend Colonel Clark spoke to him and told him the Gospel of Jesus Christ, but he refused to believe. But on La Salle Street, one of our busiest commercial streets, next day, Colonel Clark saw this same man dragging himself along on his crutches, and as he got to the entrance of an alley-way, Colonel Clark drew him into the alley-way and said to him, "My friend, Jesus has power to save you," and after talking to him a while, there and then the man got down as best he could on his crutches, beside the strong man of God, and put his trust in Jesus Christ. And when that man came out of that alley-way he came out a child of God, and he is today a preacher of the Gospel. Thank God for a Gospel that can save anybody. You cannot find me a man in all London that Jesus Christ has not power to save if he will only believe on Him. Put confidence in Him. Will you believe on the Lord Jesus Christ tonight?

# CHARLES GRANDISON FINNEY

C harles Grandison Finney was born on the 29th August 1792 in Warren, Connecticut. It was while studying to be a lawyer, that he first began to take a serious interest in the scriptures, and he was converted to Christ when he was twenty-nine years of age. He then studied for the Presbyterian ministry and in 1824 he was ordained by the Oneida Presbytery. For the next eight years he led revival meetings in upper New York State and in many major cities from Wilmington to Boston. During those years he established modern forms and methods of revivalism and was considered by many to be the forerunner of present day evangelism. He then became the minister of Chatham Street Chapel in New York City, where he was renowned for his lawyer like theological lectures, and among his best known publications are his *Lectures on Revival of Religion* (1835) and *Letters on Revival* (1845).

He was also professor at Oberlin College in Ohio, becoming second president from 1851 until 1866, and serving there until his death in 1875.

The following sermon was taken from his book *Sermons on Gospel Themes*.

Chapter Six

# CONDITIONS OF BEING SAVED

❧

*What must I do to be saved?*
- Acts16:30
❧

I bring forward this subject today not because it is new to many in this congregation, but because it is greatly needed. I am happy to know that the great inquiry of our text is beginning to be deeply and extensively agitated in this community, and under these circumstances it is the first duty of a Christian pastor to answer it, fully and plainly.

The circumstances which gave occasion to the words of the text were briefly these. Paul and Silas had gone to Philippi to preach the Gospel. Their preaching excited great opposition and tumult; they were arrested and thrown into prison, and the jailor was charged to keep them safely. At midnight they were praying and singing praises - God came down - the earth quaked and the prison rocked - its doors burst open, and their chains fell off; the jailor sprang up affrighted, and supposing his prisoners had fled, was about to take his own life, when Paul cried out, "Do thyself no harm; we are all here." He then called for a light, and sprang in and came trembling, and fell down before Paul and Silas, and brought them out and said, "Sirs, what must I do to be saved?"

This is briefly the history of our text; and I improve it now, by showing, -

> i.   *What sinners must not do to be saved; and*
> ii.  *What they must do.*

It has now come to be necessary and very important to tell men what they must *not* do in order to be saved. When the Gospel was first preached, Satan had not introduced as many delusions to mislead men as he has now. It was then enough to give, as Paul did, the simple and direct answer, telling men only what they must at once do. But this seems to be not enough now. So many delusions and perversions have bewildered and darkened the minds of men that they need often a great deal of instruction to lead them back to those simple views of the subject which prevailed at first. Hence the importance of showing what sinners must *not* do, if they intend to be saved.

*1. They must not imagine that they have nothing to do.* In Paul's time nobody seems to have thought of this. Then the doctrine of Universalism was not much developed. Men had not begun to dream that they should be saved without doing anything. They had not learned that sinners have nothing to do to be saved. If this idea, so current of late, had been rife at Philippi, the question of our text would not have been asked. No trembling sinner would have cried out, *What must I do to be saved?*

If men imagine they have nothing to do, they are never likely to be saved. It is not in the nature of falsehood and lies to save men's souls, and surely nothing is more false that this notion. *Men know they have something to do to be saved.* Why, then, do they pretend that all men will be saved whether they do their duty, or constantly refuse to do it? The very idea is preposterous, and it is entertained only by the most palpable outrage upon common sense and an enlightened conscience.

*2. You should not mistake what you have to do.* The duty required of sinners is very simple, and would be easily understood were it not for the false ideas that prevail as to what religion is, and as to the exact things which God requires as conditions of salvation. On these points erroneous opinions prevail to a most alarming extent. Hence the danger of mistake. Beware lest you be deceived in a matter of so vital moment.

*3. Do not say or imagine that you cannot do what God requires.* On the contrary, always assume that you can. If you assume that you cannot, this very assumption will be fatal to your salvation.

*4. Do not procrastinate.* As you ever intend or hope to be saved, you must set your face like a flint against this most pernicious delusion. Probably no other mode of evading present duty has ever prevailed so extensively as this, or has destroyed so many souls. Almost all men in Gospel lands intend to prepare for death - intend to repent and become religious before they die. Even Universalists expect to become religious at some time - perhaps after death - perhaps after being purified from their sins by purgatorial fires; but *somehow* they expect to become holy, for they know they *must* before they can see God and enjoy His presence. But you will observe, they put this matter of becoming holy off to the most distant time possible. Feeling a strong dislike to it now, they flatter themselves that God will take care that it shall be done up duly in the next world, howmuchsoever they may frustrate His efforts to do it in this. So long as it remains in their power to choose whether to become holy or not, they improve the time to enjoy sin; and leave it with God to make them holy in the next world - if they can't prevent it there! *Consistency is a jewel!* And all those who put off being religious now in the cherished delusion of becoming so in some future time, whether in this world or the next, are acting out this same inconsistency. You fondly hope *that* will occur which you are now doing your utmost to prevent.

So sinners by myriads press their way down to hell under this delusion. They often, when pressed with the claims of God, will even name the time when they will repent. It may be very near - perhaps as soon as they get home from the meeting, or as soon as the sermon is over; or it may be more remote, as for example, when they have finished their education, or become settled in life, or have made a little more property, or get ready to abandon some business of questionable morality; but no matter whether the time set be near or remote, the delusion is fatal - the thought of procrastination is murder to the soul. Ah, such sinners are little aware that Satan himself has poured out his spirit upon them and is leading them whithersoever he will. He little cares whether they put off for a longer time or a shorter. If he can persuade them to a long delay, he likes it well; if only to a short one, he feels quite sure he can renew the delay and get another extension - so it answers his purpose fully in the end.

Now mark, sinner, if you ever mean to be saved you must resist and grieve away this spirit of Satan. You must cease to procrastinate. You can never be converted so long as you operate only in the way of delaying and promising yourself that you will become religious at some future time. Did you ever bring anything to pass in your temporal business by procrastination? Did procrastination ever begin, prosecute, and accomplish any important business?

Suppose you have some business of vast consequence, involving your character, or your whole estate, or your life, to be transacted in Cleveland, but you do not know precisely how soon it *must* be done. It may be done with safety now, and with greater facility now than ever hereafter; but it might possibly be done although you should delay a little time, but every moment's delay involves an absolute uncertainty of your being able to do it at all. You do not know but a single hour's delay will make you too late. Now in these circumstances what would a man of sense and discretion do? Would he not be awake and up in an instant? Would he sleep on a matter of such moment, involving such risks and uncertainties? No. You know that the risk of a hundred dollars, pending on such conditions, would stir the warm blood of any man of business, and you could not tempt him to delay an hour. O, he would say, this is the great business to which I must attend, and everything else must give way. But suppose he should act as a sinner does about repentance, and promise himself that tomorrow will be as this day and much more abundant - and do nothing today, nor tomorrow, nor the next month, nor the next year - would you not think him beside himself? Would you expect his business to be done, his money to be secured, his interests to be promoted?

So the sinner accomplishes nothing but his own ruin so long as he procrastinates. Until he says - "Now is my time - *today* I will do all my duty" - he is only playing the fool and laying up his wages accordingly. O, it is infinite madness to defer a matter of such vast interest and of such perilous uncertainty!

5. If you would be saved *you must not wait for God to do what He commands you to do.*

God will surely do all that He can do for your salvation. All that the nature of the case allows of His doing, He either has done or stands ready to do as soon as your position and course will allow Him to do it. Long before you were born He anticipated your wants as a sinner, and began on the most liberal scale to make provision for them. He gave His Son to die for you, thus doing all that need be done by way of an atonement. Of a long time past He has been shaping His providence so as to give you the requisite knowledge of duty - has sent you His Word and Spirit. Indeed, He has given you the highest possible evidence that He will be energetic and prompt on His part - as one in earnest for your salvation. *You know this.* What sinner in this house fears lest God should be negligent on His part in the matter of his salvation? Not one. No, many of you are not a little annoyed that God should press you so earnestly and be so energetic in the work of securing your salvation. And now can you quiet your conscience with the excuse of waiting for God to do *your duty?*

The fact is, there are things for you to do which God cannot do for you. Those things which He has enjoined and revealed as the conditions of your salvation, He can not and will not do Himself. If He could have done them Himself, He would not have asked you to do them. Every sinner ought to consider this. God requires of you repentance and faith because it is naturally impossible that any one else but you should do them.  They are your own personal matters - the voluntary exercises of your own mind; and no other being in heaven, earth, or hell can do these things for you in your stead.  As far as substitution was naturally possible, God has introduced it, as in the case of the atonement.  He has never hesitated to march up to meet and to bear all the self-denials which the work of salvation has involved.

6. *If you mean to be saved you must not wait for God to do anything whatever.*  There is nothing to be waited for.  God has either done all on His part already, or if anything more remains, He is ready and waiting this moment for you to do your duty that He may impart all needful grace.

7. *Do not flee to any refuge of lies.*  Lies cannot save you. It is truth, not lies, that alone can save.  I have often wondered how men could suppose that Universalism could save any man.

Men must be sanctified by the truth.  There is no plainer teaching in the Bible than this, and no Bible doctrine is better sustained by reason and the nature of the case.

Now does Universalism sanctify anybody? Universalists say you must be punished for your sins, and that thus they will be put away as if the fires of purgatory would thoroughly consume all sin, and bring out the sinner pure.  Is this being sanctified by the truth? You might as well hope to be saved by eating liquid fire! You might as well expect fire to purify your soul from sin in this world, as in the next! Why not?

It is amazing that men should hope to be sanctified and saved by this great error, or, indeed, by any error whatever.  God says you must be sanctified *by the truth.*  Suppose you could believe this delusion, would it make you holy?  Do you believe that it would make you humble, heavenly-minded, sin-hating, benevolent? Can you believe any such thing?  Be assured that Satan is only the father of lies, and he can not save you, in fact, he would not if he could; he intends his lies not to save you, but to destroy your very soul, and nothing could be more adapted to its purpose.  Lies are only the natural poison of the soul.  You take them at your peril!

*8. Don't seek for any self-indulgent method of salvation.* The great effort among sinners has always been to be saved in some way of self-indulgence. They are slow to admit that self-denial is indispensable - that *total, unqualified self-denial is the condition of being saved.* I warn you against supposing that you can be saved in some easy, self-pleasing way. Men ought to know, and always assume, that it is naturally indispensable for selfishness to be utterly put away and its demands resisted and put down.

I often ask, - Does the system of salvation which I preach so perfectly chime with the intuitions of my reason that I know from within myself that this Gospel is the thing I need? Does it in all its parts and relations meet the demands of my intelligence? Are its requisitions obviously just and right? Do its prescribed conditions of salvation obviously befit man's moral position before God, and his moral relations to the government of God?]

To these and similar questions I am constrained to answer in the affirmative. The longer I live the more fully I see that the Gospel system is the only one that can alike meet the demands of the human intelligence, and supply the wants of man's sinning, depraved heart. The duties enjoined upon the sinner are just those things which I know must in the nature of the case be the conditions of salvation. Why, then, should any sinner think of being saved on any other conditions? Why desire it even if it were ever so practicable?

*9. Don't imagine you will ever have a more favourable time.*

Impenitent sinners are prone to imagine that just now is by no means so convenient a season as may be expected hereafter. So they put off in hope of a better time. They think perhaps that they shall have more conviction, and fewer obstacles, and less hindrances. So thought Felix. He did not intend to forego salvation, any more than you do; but he was very busy just then - had certain ends to be secured which seemed peculiarly pressing, and so he begged to be excused on the promise of very faithful attention to the subject at the expected convenient season. But did the convenient season ever come? Never. Nor does it ever come to those who in like manner resist God's solemn call, and grieve away His Spirit. Thousands are now waiting in the pains of hell who said just as he did "Go thy way for this time, when I have a convenient season I will call for thee." Oh, sinner, *when will your convenient season come?* Are you aware that no season will ever be *"convenient"* for you, unless God calls up your attention earnestly and solemnly to the subject? And can you expect Him to do this at the time of *your* choice, when you scorn His call at the time of *His* choice? Have you not heard Him say, "Because I have called, and ye refused, I have stretched out my hand, and no man regarded, but ye have set at nought all my counsel, and would none of my reproof; I also will laugh at your calamity; I will mock when your fear cometh. When your fear cometh as desolation, and your destruction cometh as a whirlwind, when distress and anguish cometh upon you; then shall they call upon me, but I will not answer; they shall seek me early, but they shall not find me." (Prov. 1:24-28). O sinner that will be a fearful and a final doom! And the myriad voices of God's universe will say, *amen.*

*10. Do not suppose that you will find another time as good, and one in which you can just as well repent as now.*

Many are ready to suppose that though there may be no better time for themselves, there will at least be one *as good.* Vain delusion! Sinner, you already owe ten thousand talents, and will you find it just as easy to be forgiven this debt while you are showing that you don't care how much and how long you augment it? In a case like this, where everything turns upon your securing the goodwill of your creditor, do you hope to gain it by positively insulting him to his face?

Or take another view of the case. Your heart you know must one day relent for sin, or you are forever damned. You know also that each successive sin increases the hardness of your heart, and makes it a more difficult matter to repent. How, then, can you reasonably hope that a future time will be equally favorable for your repentance? When you have hardened your neck like an iron sinew, and made your heart like an adamant stone, can you hope that repentance will yet be as easy to you as ever?

You know sinner that God requires you to break off from your sins *now.* But you look up into His face, and say to Him "Lord, it is just as well to stop abusing Thee at some future convenient time. Lord, if I can only be saved at last, I shall think it all my gain to go on insulting and abusing Thee as long as it will possibly answer. And since Thou art so very compassionate and long-suffering, I think I may venture on in sin and rebellion against Thee yet these many months and years longer. Lord, don't hurry me - do let me have my way; let me abuse Thee if Thou pleasest, and spit in Thy face - all will be just as well if I only repent in season so as finally to be saved. I know, indeed, that Thou art entreating me to repent now, but I much prefer to wait a season and it will be just as well to repent at some future time."

And now do you suppose that God will set His seal to this - that He will say "You are right, sinner, I set my seal of approbation upon your course - it is well that you take so just views of your duty to your Maker and your Father; go on; your course will ensure your salvation." Do you expect such a response from God as this?

*11. If you ever expect to be saved, don't wait to see what others will do or say.*

I was lately astonished to find that a young lady here under conviction was in great trouble about what a beloved brother would think of her if she should give her heart to God. She knew her duty; but he was impenitent, and how could she know what he would think if she should repent now! It amounts to this. She would come before God and say "O Thou great God, I know I ought to repent, but I can't; for I don't know as my brother will like it. I know that he too is a sinner, and must repent or lose his soul, but I am much more afraid of his frown than I am of Thine, and I care more for his approbation than I do for Thine, and consequently, I dare not repent till he does!" How shocking is this! Strange that on such a subject men will ever ask, "What will others say of me?" Are you amenable to God? What, then, have others to say about your duty to Him? God requires you and them also to repent, *and why don't you do it at once?*

Not long since, as I was preaching abroad, one of the principal men of the city came to the meeting for inquiry, apparently much convicted and in great distress for his soul. But being a man of high political standing, and supposing himself to be very dependent upon his friends, he insisted that he must consult them, and have a regard for their feelings in this matter. I could not possibly beat him off from this ground, although I spent three hours in the effort. He seemed almost ready to repent - I thought he certainly would; but he slipped away, relapsed by a perpetual backsliding, and I expect will be found at last among the lost in perdition. Would you not expect such a result if he tore himself away under such an excuse as that?

O sinner, you must not care what others say of you, let them say what they please. Remember, the question is between your own soul and God, and "He that is wise shall be wise for himself, and he that scorneth, he alone shall bear it." You must die for yourself, and for yourself must appear before God in judgment! Go, young woman, ask your brother "Can you answer for me when I come to the judgment? Can you pledge yourself that you can stand in my stead and answer for me there?" Now until you have reason to believe that he can, it is wise for you to disregard his opinions if they stand at all in your way. Whoever interposes any objection to your immediate repentance, fail not to ask him, "Can you shield my soul in the judgment? If I can be assured that you can and will, I will make you my Saviour; but if not, then I must attend to my own salvation, and leave you to attend to yours."

I never shall forget the scene that occurred while my own mind was turning upon this great point. Seeking a retired place for prayer, I went into a deep grove, found a perfectly secluded spot behind some large logs, and knelt down. All suddenly, a leaf rustled and I sprang, for somebody must be coming and I shall be seen here at prayer. I had not been aware that I cared what others said of me, but looking back upon my exercises of mind here, I could see that I did care infinitely too much what others thought of me.

Closing my eyes again for prayer, I heard a rustling leaf again, and then the thought came over me like a wave of the sea, "I *am* ashamed of confessing my sin!" What! thought I, ashamed of being found speaking with God! O, how ashamed I felt of this shame! I can never describe the strong and overpowering impression, which this thought made on my mind. I cried aloud at the very top of my voice, for I felt that though all the men on earth and all the devils in hell were present to hear and see me I would not shrink and would not cease to cry unto God; for what is it to me if others see me seeking the face of my God and Saviour? I am fastening to the judgment: - *there* I shall not be ashamed to have the judge my friend. *There* I shall not be ashamed to have sought His face and His pardon here. *There* will be no shrinking away from the gaze of the universe. O, if sinners at the judgment could shrink away, how gladly would they; but they cannot! Nor can they stand there in each other's places to answer for each other's sins. That young woman, can she say then - O, my brother, you must answer for me; for to please you, I rejected Christ and lost my soul? That brother is himself a guilty rebel, confounded, and agonized, and quailing before the awful judge, and how can he befriend you in such an awful hour! Fear not his displeasure now, but rather warn him while you can, to escape for his life ere the wrath of the Lord wax hot against him, and there be no remedy.

12. If you would be saved, *you must not indulge prejudices against either God, or His ministers, or against Christians, or against anything religious.*

There are some persons of peculiar temperament who are greatly in danger of losing their souls because they are tempted to strong prejudices. Once committed, either in favor of or against any persons or things, they are exceedingly apt to become so fixed as never more to be really honest. And when these persons or things in regard to which they become committed, are so connected with religion, that their prejudices stand arrayed against their fulfilling the great conditions of salvation, the effect can be nothing else than ruinous. For it is naturally indispensable to salvation that you should be entirely honest. Your soul must act before God in the open sincerity of truth, or you cannot be converted.

I have known persons in revivals to remain a long time under great conviction, without submitting themselves to God, and by careful inquiry I have found them wholly hedged in by their prejudices, and yet so blind to this fact that they would not admit that they had any prejudice at all. In my observation of convicted sinners, I have found this among the most common obstacles in the way of the salvation of souls. Men become committed against religion, and remaining in this state it is naturally impossible that they should repent. God will not humor your prejudices, or lower His prescribed conditions of salvation to accommodate your feelings.

Again, you must give up all hostile feelings in cases where you have been really injured. Sometimes I have seen persons evidently shut out from the kingdom of heaven, because having been really injured, they would not forgive and forget, but maintained such a spirit of resistance and revenge, that they could not, in the nature of the case, repent of the sin toward God, nor could God forgive them. Of course they lost heaven. I have heard men say "I can not forgive - I will not forgive – I have been injured, and I never will forgive that wrong" Now mark: you must not hold on to such feelings; if you do, you cannot be saved.

Again, you must not suffer yourself to be stumbled by the prejudices of others. I have often been struck with the state of things in families, where the parents or older persons had prejudices against the minister, and have wondered why those parents were not more wise than to lay stumbling-blocks before their children to ruin their souls. This is often the true reason why children are not converted. Their minds are turned against the Gospel, by being turned against those from whom they hear it preached. I would rather have persons come into my family, and curse and swear before my children, than to have them speak against those who preach to them the Gospel. Therefore I say to all parents take care what you say, if you would not shut the gate of heaven against your children!

Again, do not allow yourself to take some fixed position, and then suffer the stand you have taken to debar you from doing any obvious duty. Persons sometimes allow themselves to be committed against taking what is called "the anxious seat;" and consequently they refuse to go forward under circumstances when it is obviously proper that they should, and where their refusal to do so, places them in an attitude unfavorable, and perhaps fatal to their conversion. Let every sinner beware of this!

Again, do not hold on to anything about which you have any doubt of its lawfulness or propriety. Cases often occur in which persons are not fully satisfied that a thing is wrong, and yet are not satisfied that it is right. Now in cases of this sort it should not be enough to say, "such and such Christians do so;" you ought to have better reasons than this for your course of conduct. If you ever expect to be saved, you must abandon all practices which you even suspect to be wrong. This principle seems to be involved in the passage, "He that doubteth is damned if he eat; for whatsoever is not of faith is sin." To do that which is of doubtful propriety is to allow yourself to tamper with the divine authority, and cannot fail to break down in your mind that solemn dread of sinning which, if you would ever be saved, you must carefully cherish.

Again, if you would be saved, do not look at professors and wait for them to become engaged as they should be in the great work of God. If they are not what they ought to be, let them alone. Let them bear their own awful responsibility. It often happens that convicted sinners compare themselves with professed Christians, and excuse themselves for delaying their duty, because professed Christians are delaying theirs. Sinners must not do this if they would ever be saved. It is very probable that you will always find guilty professors enough to stumble over into hell if you will allow yourself to do so.

But on the other hand, many professors may not be nearly so bad as you suppose, and you must not be censorious, putting the worst construction upon their conduct. You have other work to do than this. Let them stand or fall to their own master. Unless you abandon the practice of picking flaws in the conduct of professed Christians, it is utterly impossible that you should be saved.

Again, do not depend upon professors on their prayers or influence in any way. I have known children hang a long time upon the prayers of their parents, putting those prayers in the place of Jesus Christ, or at least in the place of their own present efforts to do their duty. Now this course pleases Satan entirely. He would ask nothing more to make sure of you. Therefore, depend on no prayers, not even those of the holiest Christians on earth. The matter of your conversion lies between yourself and God alone, as really as if you were the only sinner in the world, or as if there were no other beings in the universe but yourself and your God.

Do not *seek for any apology* or *excuse whatever.* I dwell upon this and urge it the more because I so often find persons resting on some excuse without being themselves aware of it. In conversation with them upon their spiritual state, I see this and say, "There you are resting on that excuse." "Am I?" say they, "I did not know it."

Do not seek for stumbling-blocks. Sinners, a little disturbed in their stupidity, begin to cast about for stumbling-blocks for self-vindication. All at once they become wide awake to the faults of professors, as if they had to bear the care of all the churches. The real fact is they are all engaged to find something to which they can take exception, so that they can thereby blunt the keen edge of truth upon their own consciences. This never helps along their own salvation.

Do not tempt the forbearance of God. If you do, you are in the utmost danger of being given over forever. Do not presume that you may go on yet longer in your sins, and still find the gate of mercy. This resumption has paved the way for the ruin of many souls.

Do not despair of salvation and settle down in unbelief, saying, "There is no mercy for me." You must not despair in any such sense as to shut yourself out from the kingdom. You may well despair of being saved without Christ and without repentance; but you are bound to believe the Gospel; and to do this is to believe the glad tidings that Jesus Christ has come to save sinners, even the chief, and that "Him that cometh to Him He will in no wise cast out." You have no right to disbelieve this, and act as if there were no truth in it.

You must not wait for more conviction. Why do you need any more? You know your guilt and know your present duty. Nothing can be more preposterous, therefore, than to wait for more conviction. If you did not know that you are a sinner, or that you are guilty for sin, there might be some fitness in seeking for conviction of the truth on these points.

Do not wait for more or for different feelings. Sinners are often saying, "I must feel differently before I can come to Christ," or "I must have *more* feeling." As if this were the great thing which God requires of them. In this they are altogether mistaken.

Do not wait to be better prepared. While you wait you are growing worse and worse, and are fast rendering your salvation impossible.

Don't wait for God to change your heart. Why should you wait for

Him to do what He has commanded you to do, and waits for you to do in obedience to His command?

Don't try to recommend yourself to God by prayers or tears or by anything else whatsoever. Do you suppose your prayers lay God under any obligation to forgive you? Suppose you owed a man five hundred talents, and should go a hundred times a week and beg him to remit to you this debt; and then should enter your prayers in account against your creditor, as so much claim against him. Suppose you should pursue this course till you had cancelled the debt, as you suppose - could you hope to prove anything by this course except that you were mad? And yet sinners seem to suppose that their many prayers and tears lay the Lord under real obligation to them to forgive them.

Never rely on anything else whatever than Jesus Christ, and Him crucified. It is preposterous for you to hope, as many do, to make some propitiation by your own sufferings. In my early experience I thought I could not expect to be converted at once, but must be bowed down a long time. I said to myself, "God will not pity me till I feel worse than I do now. I can't expect Him to forgive me till I feel a greater agony of soul than this." Now even if I could have gone on augmenting my sufferings till they equalled the miseries of hell, it could not have changed God. The fact is, God does not ask of you that you should suffer. Your sufferings cannot in the nature of the case avail for atonement. Why, therefore, should you attempt to thrust aside the system of God's providing, and thrust in one of your own?

There is another view of the case. The thing God demands of you is that you should bow your stubborn will to Him just as a child in the attitude of disobedience, and required to submit, might fall to weeping and groaning, and to every expression of agony, and might even torture himself, in hope of moving the pity of his father, but all the time refuses to submit to parental authority. He would be very glad to put his own sufferings in the place of the submission demanded. This is what the sinner is doing. He would fain put his own sufferings in the place of submission to God, and move the pity of the Lord so much that He would recede from the hard condition of repentance and submission.

If you would be saved you must not listen at all to those who pity you, and who impliedly take your part against God, and try to make you think you are not so bad as you are. I once knew a woman who after a long season of distressing conviction fell into great despair, her health sank, and she seemed about to die. All this time she found no relief, but seemed only to wax worse and worse, sinking down in stern and awful despair. Her friends instead of dealing plainly and faithfully with her, and probing her guilty heart to the bottom, had taken the course of pitying her, and almost complained of the Lord that He would not have compassion on the poor agonized, dying woman. At length, as she seemed in the last stages of life, so weak as to be scarcely able to speak in a low voice, there happened in a minister who better understood how to deal with convicted sinners. The woman's friends cautioned him to deal very carefully with her, as she was in a dreadful state and greatly to be pitied; but he judged it best to deal with her very faithfully. As he approached her bedside, she raised her faint voice and begged for a little water. "Unless you repent, you will soon be," said he, "where there is not a drop of water to cool your tongue." "O," she cried, *"must I go down to hell?"* "Yes, you must, and you will, soon, unless you repent and submit to God. Why don't you repent and submit immediately?" "O," she replied, "it is an awful thing to go to hell!" "Yes, and for that very reason God has provided an atonement through Jesus Christ, but *you won't accept it.* He brings the cup of salvation to your lips, and you thrust it away. Why will you do this? Why will you persist in being an enemy of God and scorn His offered salvation, when you might become His friend and have His salvation if you would?" This was the strain of their conversation, and its result was, that the woman saw her guilt and her duty, and turning to the Lord, found pardon and peace.

Therefore, I say if your conscience convicts you of sin, don't let anybody take your part against God. Your wound needs not a plaster, but a *probe.* Don't fear the probe; it is the only thing that can save you. Don't seek to hide your guilt, or veil your eyes from seeing it, nor be afraid to know the worst, for you must know the very worst, and the sooner you know it the better. I warn you, don't look after some physician to give you an opiate, for you don't need it. Shun, as you would death itself, all those who would speak to you smooth things and prophesy deceits. They would surely ruin your soul.

Again, do not suppose that if you become a Christian, it will interfere with any of the necessary or appropriate duties of life, or with anything whatever to which you ought to attend. No, religion never interferes with any real duty. So far is this from being the case, that in fact a proper attention to your various duties is indispensable to your being religious. You cannot serve God without.

Moreover, if you would be saved you must not give heed to anything that would hinder you. It is infinitely important that your soul should be saved. No consideration thrown in your way should be allowed to have the weight of a straw or a feather. Jesus Christ has illustrated and enforced this by several parables, especially in the one which compares the kingdom of heaven to "a merchant-man seeking goodly pearls, who when he had found one pearl of great price went and sold all that he had and bought it." In another parable, the kingdom of heaven is said to be "like treasure hid in a field, which, when a man hath found, he hideth, and for joy thereof goeth and selleth all that he hath and buyeth that field." Thus forcibly are men taught that they must be ready to make any sacrifice whatever which may be requisite in order to gain the kingdom of heaven.

Again, you *must not seek religion selfishly.* You must not make your own salvation or happiness the supreme end. Beware, for if you make this your supreme end you will get a false hope, and will probably glide along down the pathway of the hypocrite into the deepest hell.

## II. *What sinners must do to be saved.*

1. *You must understand what you have to do.*

It is of the utmost importance that you should see this clearly. You need to know that you must return to God, and to understand what this means. The difficulty between yourself and God is that you have stolen yourself and run away from His service. You belong of right to God. He created you for Himself, and hence had a perfectly righteous claim to the homage of your heart, and the service of your life. But you, instead of living to meet His claims, have run away - have deserted from God's service, and have lived to please yourself. Now your duty is to return and restore yourself to God.

*2. You must return and confess your sins to God.*

You must confess that you have been all wrong, and that God has been all right. Go before the Lord and lay open the depth of your guilt. Tell Him you deserve just as much damnation as He has threatened.

These confessions are naturally indispensable to your being forgiven. In accordance with this the Lord says, "If then their uncircumcised hearts be humbled, and they then *accept of the punishment* of their iniquity, then will I remember my covenant." Then God can forgive. But so long as you controvert this point, and will not concede that God is right, or admit that you are wrong, He can never forgive you.

You must moreover confess to man if you have injured any one. And is it not a fact that you have injured some, and perhaps many of your fellow-men? Have you not slandered your neighbor and said things which you have no right to say? Have you not in some instances, which you could call to mind if you would, lied to them, or about them, or covered up or perverted the truth; and have you not been willing that others should have false impressions of you or of your conduct? If so, you must renounce all such iniquity, for "He that covereth his sins shall not prosper; while he that confesseth and forsaketh them shall find mercy." And, furthermore, you must not only confess your sins to God and to the men you have injured, but you must also *make restitution.* You have not taken the position of a penitent before God and man until you have done this also. God cannot treat you as a penitent until you have done it. I do not mean by this that God can not forgive you until you have carried into effect your purpose of restitution by finishing the outward act, for sometimes it may demand time, and may in some cases be itself impossible to you. But the purpose must be sincere and thorough before you can be forgiven of God.

3. *You must renounce yourself.* In this is implied -

(a.) That you renounce your own righteousness, forever discarding the very idea of having any righteousness in yourself.

(b.) That you forever relinquish the idea of *having done any good* which ought to commend you to God, or be ever thought of as a ground of your justification.

(c.) That you *renounce your own will,* and be ever ready to say not in word only, but in heart "Thy will be done, on earth as it is in heaven." You must consent most heartily that God's will shall be your supreme law.

(d.) That you renounce *your own way* and let God have His own way in everything. Never suffer yourself to fret and be rasped by anything whatever; for since God's agency extends to all events, you ought to recognize His hand in all things; and of course to fret at anything whatever is to fret against God who has at least *permitted* that thing to occur as it does. So long, therefore as you suffer yourself to fret, you are not right with God. You must become before God as a little child, subdued and trustful at His feet. Let the weather be fair or foul, consent that God should have His way. Let all things go well with you, or as men call it, *ill;* yet let God do His pleasure, and let it be your part to submit in perfect resignation. Until you take this ground you cannot be saved.

4. *You must come to Christ.*

You must accept of Christ really and fully *as your Saviour.* Renouncing all thought of depending on anything you have done or can do, you must accept of Christ as your atoning sacrifice, and as your ever-living Mediator before God. Without the least qualification or reserve you must place yourself under His wing as your Saviour.

5. *You must seek supremely to please Christ, and not yourself.*

It is naturally impossible that you should be saved until you come into this attitude of mind - until you are so well pleased with Christ in all respects as to find your pleasure in doing His. It is in the nature of things impossible that you should be happy in any other state of mind, or unhappy in this. For, His pleasure is infinitely good and right. When, therefore, His good pleasure becomes your good pleasure, and your will harmonizes entirely with His, then you will be happy for the same reason that He is happy, and you cannot fail of being happy any more than Jesus Christ can. And this becoming supremely happy in God's will is essentially the idea of salvation. In this state of mind *you are saved.* Out of it you cannot be.

It has often struck my mind with great force, that many professors of religion are deplorably and utterly mistaken on this point. Their real feeling is that Christ's service is an iron collar - an insufferably hard yoke. Hence, they labor exceedingly to throw off some of this burden. They try to make it out that Christ does not require much, if any, self-denial - much, if any, deviation from the course of worldliness and sin. O, if they could only get the standard of Christian duty quite down to a level with the fashions and customs of this world! How much easier then to live a Christian life and wear Christ's yoke!

But taking Christ's yoke as it really is, it becomes in their view an iron collar. Doing the will of Christ, instead of their own, is a hard business. Now if doing Christ's will *is* religion, (and who can doubt it?) then they only need enough of it; and *in their state of mind* they will be supremely wretched. Let me ask those who groan under the idea that they *must* be religious - who deem it awful hard - but they *must* - how much religion of this kind would it take to make hell? Surely not much! When it gives you no joy to do God's pleasure, and yet you are shut up to the doing of His pleasure as the only way to be saved, and are thereby perpetually dragooned into the doing of what you hate, as the only means of escaping hell, would not this be itself a hell? Can you not see that in this state of mind you are not saved and cannot be?

To be saved you must come into a state of mind in which you will ask no higher joy than to do God's pleasure. This alone will be forever enough to fill your cup to overflowing.

*6. You must have all confidence in Christ, or you cannot be saved.*

You must absolutely believe in Him - believe all His words of promise. They were given you to be believed, and unless you believe them they can do you no good at all. So far from helping you without you exercise faith in them, they will only aggravate your guilt for unbelief. God would be believed when He speaks in love to lost sinners. He gave them these "exceeding great and precious promises, that they, by faith in them, might escape the corruption that is in the world through lust." But thousands of professors of religion know not how to use these promises, and as to them or any profitable use *they make,* the promises might as well have been written on the sands of the sea.

Sinners, too, will go down to hell in unbroken masses, unless they believe and take hold of God by faith in His promise. O, His awful wrath is out against them! And He says, "I would go through them, I would burn them up together; *or let him take hold of My strength,* that he may make peace with Me, and he shall make peace with Me." Yes, let him stir up himself and take hold of My arm, strong to save, and then he may make peace with Me. Do you ask how take hold? By faith. Yes, *by faith;* believe His words and *take hold;* take hold of His strong arm and swing right out over hell, and don't be afraid any more than if there were no hell.

But you say - "I do believe, and yet I am not saved." No, you don't believe. A woman said to me, "I believe, I know I do, and yet here I am in my sins." No, said I, you don't. Have you as much confidence in God as you would have in me if I had promised you a dollar? Do you ever pray to God? And, if so, do you come with any such confidence as you would have if you came to me to ask for a promised dollar? Oh, until you have as much faith in God as this, aye and more - until you have more confidence in God than you would have in ten thousand men, your faith does not honor God, and you cannot hope to please Him. You must say - "Let God be true though every man be a liar."

But you say - "O, I am a sinner, and how can I believe?" I know you are a sinner, and so are all men to whom God has given these promises. "O, but I am a *great sinner!*" Well, "It is a faithful saying and worthy of all acceptation, that Christ Jesus came into the world to save sinners, of whom," Paul says, "I am the chief." So you need not despair.

7. *You must forsake all that you have,* or you cannot be Christ's disciple. There must be absolute and total self-denial.

By this I do not mean that you are never to eat again, or never again to clothe yourself, or never more enjoy the society of your friends - no, not this; but that you should cease entirely from using any of these enjoyments selfishly. You must no longer think to own yourself - your time, your possessions, or anything you have ever called your own. All these things you must hold as God's, not yours. In this sense you are to forsake all that you have, namely, in the sense of laying all upon God's altar to be devoted supremely and only to His service. When you come back to God for pardon and salvation, come with all you have to lay all at His feet. Come with your body, to offer it as a living sacrifice upon His altar. Come with your soul and all its powers, and yield them in willing consecration to your God and Saviour. Come, bring them all along - everything, body, soul, intellect, imagination, acquirements - all, without reserve. Do you say - Must I bring them all? Yes, all - absolutely ALL; do not keep back anything - don't sin against your own soul, like Ananias and Sapphira, by keeping back a part, but renounce your own claim to everything, and recognize God's right to all. Say - Lord, these things are not mine. I had stolen them, but they were never mine. They were always Thine; I'll have them no longer. Lord, these things are all Thine, henceforth and forever. Now, what wilt Thou have me to do? I have no business of my own to do I am wholly at Thy disposal. Lord, what work hast Thou for me to do?

In this spirit you must renounce the world, the flesh, and Satan. Your fellowship is henceforth to be with Christ, and not with those objects. You are to live for Christ, and not for the world, the flesh, or the devil.

8. *You must believe the record God hath given of His Son.* He that believes not does not receive the record - does not set to his seal that

God is true. "This is the record that God has given us eternal life, and this life is in His Son." The condition of your having it is that you believe the record, and of course that you act accordingly. Suppose here is a poor man living at your next door, and the mail brings him a letter stating that a rich man has died in England, leaving him £100,000, and the cashier of a neighboring bank writes him that he has received the amount on deposit for him, and holds it subject to his order. Well, the poor man says, I can't believe the record. I can't believe there ever was any such rich man; I can't believe there is £100,000 for me. So he must live and die as poor as Lazarus, because he won't believe the record.

Now, mark; this is just the case with the unbelieving sinner. God has given you eternal life, and it waits your order; but you don't get it because you will not believe, and therefore will not make out the order, and present in due form the application.

Ah, but you say, I must have some feeling before I can believe - how can I believe till I have the feeling? So the poor man might say - How can I believe that the £100,000 is mine; I have not got a farthing of it now; I am as poor as ever. Yes, you are poor because you *will* not *believe*. *If* you would believe, you might go and buy out every store in this country. Still you cry - I am as poor as ever. I can't believe it; see my poor worn clothes - I was never more ragged in my life; I have not a particle of the feeling and the comforts of a rich man. So the sinner can't believe till he gets the inward experience! He must wait to have some of the feeling of a saved sinner before he can believe the record and take hold of the salvation! Preposterous enough! So the poor man must wait to get his new clothes and fine house before he can believe his documents and draw for his money. Of course he dooms himself to everlasting poverty, although mountains of gold were all his own.

Now, sinner, you must understand this. Why should you be lost when eternal life is bought and offered you by the last will and testament of the Lord Jesus Christ? Will you not believe the record and draw for the amount at once! Do for mercy's sake understand this and not lose heaven by your own folly!

I must conclude by saying, that if you would be saved you must accept a *prepared salvation,* one already prepared and full, and present. You must be willing to give up all your sins, and be saved from them, *all, now and henceforth.* Until you consent to this, you cannot be saved at all. Many would be willing to be saved in heaven, if they might hold on to some sins while on earth - or rather they *think* they would like heaven on such terms. But the fact is, they would as much dislike a pure heart and a holy life in heaven as they do on earth, and they deceive themselves utterly in supposing that they are ready or even willing to go to such a heaven as God has prepared for His people. No, there can be no heaven except for those who accept a salvation *from all sin* in this world. They must take the Gospel as a system which holds no compromise with sin - which contemplates full deliverance from sin even now, and makes provision accordingly. Any other gospel is not the true one, and to accept of Christ's Gospel in any other sense is not to accept it all. Its first and its last condition is *sworn and eternal renunciation of all sin.*

### REMARKS.

1. Paul did not give the same answer to this question which a consistent Universalist would give. The latter would say, You are to be saved by being first punished according to your sin. All men must expect to be punished all that their sins deserve. But Paul did not answer thus. Miserable comforter had he been if he had answered after this sort: "You must all be punished according to the letter of the law you have broken." This could scarcely have been called *gospel.*

Nor again did Paul give the Universalist's answer and say, "Do not concern yourself about this matter of being saved; all men are sure enough of being saved without any particular anxiety about it." Not so Paul; no - he understood and did not forbear to express the necessity of believing on the Lord Jesus Christ as the condition of being saved.

2. Take care that you do not sin willfully after having understood the truth concerning the way of salvation. Your danger of this is great precisely in proportion as you see your duty clearly. The most

terrible damnation must fall on the head of those who "knew their duty, but who did it not." When, therefore, you are told plainly and truly what your duty is, be on your guard lest you let salvation slip out of your hands. It may never come so near your reach again.

3. Do not wait, even to go home, before you obey God. Make up your mind now, at once, to close in with the offers of salvation. Why not? Are they not most reasonable?

4. Let your mind act upon this great proposal and embrace it just as you would any other important proposition. God lays the proposition before you; you hear it explained, and you understand it; now the next and only remaining step is - to *embrace it with all your heart*. Just as any other great question (we may suppose it a question of life or death) might come before a community - the case be fully stated, the conditions explained, and then the issue is made. *Will you subscribe?* Will you engage to meet these conditions? Do you heartily embrace the proposition? Now all this would be intelligible.

Just so, now, in the case of the sinner. You understand the proposition. You know the conditions of salvation. You understand the contract into which you are to enter with your God and Saviour. You covenant to give your all to God - to lay yourself upon His altar to be used up there just as He pleases to use you. And now the only remaining question is, *Will you consent to this at once?* Will you go for full and everlasting consecration *with all your heart?*

5. The jailor made no excuse. When he knew his duty, in a moment he yielded. Paul told him what to do, and be did it. Possibly he might have heard something about Paul's preaching before this night; but probably not much. But now he hears for his life. How often have I been struck with this case! There was a dark-minded heathen. He had heard, we must suppose, a great deal of slang about these apostles; but notwithstanding all, he came to them for truth; bearing, he is convinced, and being convinced, he yields at once. Paul uttered a single sentence - he received it, embraced it, and it is done.

Now you, sinner, know and admit all this truth, and yet infinitely strange as it is, you will not, in a moment, believe and embrace it with all your heart. O, will not Sodom and Gomorrah rise up against you in the judgment and condemn you! That heathen jailor - how could you bear to see him on that dread day, and stand rebuked by his example there!

6. It is remarkable that Paul said nothing about the jailor needing any help in order to believe and repent. He did not even mention the work of the Spirit, or allude to the jailor's need of it. But it should be noticed that Paul gave the jailor just those directions which would most effectually secure the Spirit's aid and promote his action.

7. The jailor seems to have made no delay at all, waiting for no future or better time; but as soon as the conditions are before him he yields and embraces; no sooner is the proposition made than he seizes upon it in a moment.

I was once preaching in a village in New York, and there sat before me a lawyer who had been greatly offended with the Gospel. But that day I noticed he sat with fixed eye and open mouth, leaned forward as if he would seize each word as it came. I was explaining and simplifying the Gospel, and when I came to state just how the Gospel is offered to men, he said to me afterwards: I snatched at it - I put out my hand, (suiting the action to the thought), and *seized it* - and it became mine.

So in my own case while in the woods praying, after I had burst away from the fear of man, and began to give scope to my feelings this passage fell upon me, "Ye shall seek for Me and find Me when ye search for Me with all your heart." For the first time in the world I found that I *believed* before, but surely never before as I now did. Now, said I to Myself - "This is the word of the everlasting God. My God, I take Thee at Thy word. Thou sayest I shall find Thee when I search for Thee, I know, with all my heart, and now, Lord, I do search for Thee, I know, with all my heart." And true enough, I did find the Lord. Never in all my life was I more certain of anything than I was then that I had found the Lord.

This is the very idea of His promises – they were made *to be believed - to* be laid hold of as God's own words, and acted upon as if they actually meant just what they say. When God says, "Look unto Me and be ye saved," He would have us look unto Him as if He really had salvation in His hands to give, and withal a heart to give it. The true spirit of faith is well expressed by the Psalmist - "When Thou saidst – 'Seek ye my face,' my heart replied – 'Thy face, Lord, will I seek.'" This is the way - let your heart at once respond to the blessed words of invitation and of promise.

Ah, but you say, I am not a Christian. And you never will be till you believe on the Lord Jesus Christ as your Saviour. If you never become a Christian, the reason will be because you do not and will not believe the Gospel and embrace it with all your heart.

The promises were made to be believed, and belong to any one who will believe them. They reach forth their precious words to all, and whoever will, may take them as his own. Now will you believe that the Father has given you eternal life? This is the fact declared; will you believe it?

You have now been told what you must not do and what you must do to be saved; *are you prepared to act?* Do you say, I am ready to renounce my own pleasure, and henceforth seek no other pleasure than to please God? Can you forego everything else for the sake of this?

Sinner, do you want to please God, or would you choose to please yourself? Are you willing now to please God and to begin by believing on the Lord Jesus Christ unto salvation? Will you be as simple-hearted as the jailor was? And act as promptly?

I demand your decision now. I dare not have you go home first, lest you get to talking about something else, and let slip these words of life and this precious opportunity to grasp an offered salvation. And whom do you suppose I am now addressing? Every impenitent sinner in this house – *every one*. I call heaven and earth to record that I have set the Gospel before you today. *Will you take it?* Is it not reasonable for you to decide at once? Are you ready, now, to say before high heaven and before this congregation - "I will renounce myself and yield to God! I am the Lord's, and let all men and angels bear me witness – I am forevermore the Lord's." Sinner, the infinite God waits for your consent!

# J. SIDLOW BAXTER

❧

J. Sidlow Baxter was born in Sydney, Australia, and was brought to England in his childhood. He was converted to Christ at an early age, and he trained for the ministry at Spurgeon's College, London.

After twenty-five years in the pastorate, eighteen of which were spent in Scotland as pastor of Charlotte Chapel, Edinburgh, Dr. Baxter went into a wider ministry as a Bible teacher and conference speaker, both in Great Britain and the United States. The Central Baptist Seminary, Toronto, Canada, conferred the Doctor of Divinity degree on him.

He became known among evangelicals all over the English speaking world as preacher, lecturer and author.

Among his best known books are: *Explore the Book; Awake My Heart; His Part and Ours; Mark these Men; The Best Word Ever and 'Enter Ye In'* - from which this sermon is taken.

# Chapter Seven

# THE INSISTENT QUESTION

☙

*What must I do to be saved?*
- Acts 16:30

☙

Ever since the dawn of history man has been asking questions. What is the explanation behind the astronomer's telescope, but that man is asking questions about the stellar regions? What is the explanation behind the geologists' hammer, but that man is asking questions about the earth on which he lives? What is the explanation behind the archaeologist's spade, but that man is asking questions about his past? What is the explanation behind every branch of scientific enquiry and every department of intellectual culture, but that man is asking questions?

Man's Biggest Questions

But man's greatest questions are ever those that concern his moral and spiritual nature; and man has ever felt this to be so. This takes our thoughts to the Bible. Just because the Bible is the most human book in the world, we find in it the greatest moral and spiritual questions the human heart has ever asked. The Bible, however, is also the inspired word of God, and in it therefore, we find the Divine answer to the human heart.

The biggest questions of the human heart are not those that garb themselves in the slowly pondered phraseology of the philosopher, or in the technically exact terminology of the mathematician. The more deeply and honestly the human heart speaks of itself and its problems, the more does it express itself with a simplicity of speech which is native to the deepest and most real within us, so that the profounder the question the simpler is the language. Even so, the great questions of the Bible are not questions which are the outcome of long-drawn-out processes of philosophical reasoning, or tediously worked out mathematical calculations, but those which have been wrung from souls in some desperate extremity, or in some experience which has suddenly faced them with the deepest realities of life; and sometimes those who have given utterance to the great, representative, universal questions of the human heart have not realized the greatness of the questions they have asked.

## The Question Of All Questions

All this is true of that great, vital, urgent question *"What must I do to be saved?"* It was asked, not by a philosopher or a mathematician, but by a jailor, a jailor who, like all the philosophers and mathematicians, and like all the rest of us, was a sinner needing to be saved from sin. The question was asked nineteen hundred years ago, at midnight, in the old prison house at Philippi, by a man who suddenly found himself in desperate straits. Aye, but this question was asked centuries before ever the Son of God became incarnate: and it has been asked all down the course of history, in differing words and ways; and it is being asked, in varying speech, all over the world today. Hark back to ancient Confucianism, Buddhism, Hinduism; to the aboriginal religions of mankind; and you find the question everywhere. This is a universal cry of the human heart. God still lives! Conscience still speaks! Sin is still sin! God says so. Conscience says so. Man, deep in his heart, *knows* it to be so, and still cries: *"What must I do to be saved?"* He may stifle the cry. He may put himself off with all sorts of excuses. Yet he cannot utterly kill the buried anxiety of his soul. It is buried alive! - and at each crisis of his life it haunts him with its cry - "What must I do to be saved?" Why will men be such fools? Deep in our hearts we know our need; and many of us know where the need may be fully and finally dealt with; but we are too proud to come as penitent sinners for salvation; so - we become spiritual suicides.

## The Greatest Thing Of All

It is a great thing - it is the greatest thing of all, to be right with God, to be a saved soul, and to know it. The salvation of the soul is our dire need as members of a fallen race. All of us have sinned, not merely in a vague, general, "couldn't be helped" and "doesn't matter much" way; but deeply and grievously, and in a way which justly brings down the condemnation of God upon us. We are each held responsible to God. What saith the Scripture? "Every one of us shall give account of himself to God"! As truly as God is righteous, it will go hard at last with those who are without Christ.

It is a great thing indeed to be saved from the *punishment* of sin; to receive the gracious forgiveness of God through Jesus Christ, and to know that God's dear Son made full atonement for our sin on Calvary. It is a great thing indeed to be saved from the *power* of sin; for all men and women who are without Christ are slaves to sin in one form or another. When Christ comes into the heart He "breaks the power of cancelled sin." He "sets the prisoner free"! It is a great thing indeed to live one's life in conscious favour and fellowship with God, and to have the sense of His forgiving love filling the heart with peace.

Multitudes of people today neglect the salvation of their souls, and banish from their minds all thought of their accountability to God. Those of us who have fled for refuge to Christ and have come to know the glorious reality of salvation in Him, may well feel concern about the prevailing unconcern today; yet we need not feel surprised at it, for the Scriptures plainly predict that this turning away from the truth of God is to characterize these closing days of the present age.

The Spirit of God has not yet ceased to strive with men and women, however. Amid the multitudes, all around us, there are great numbers of people who, if they did but confess it, have been awakened to their sense of need, and are longing to know the secret of a right relationship with God, longing to find ease of mind, longing to find the way of salvation for their souls.

## Momentous Issues

O friend, if God's Spirit has wrought anxiety within you about the welfare of your soul, then give yourself no rest until you have found peace with God. No tongue can tell, no pen can describe, the momentousness of the issues which are involved. You are being aroused from your long slumber of spiritual death. The Spirit of God is striving with you that you may be eternally saved. God is seeking to draw you to Himself with the silken bands of His redeeming love. The hand that bears the nail-scar is knocking at your door. Heaven is bending over you in gracious entreaty. O that you may be wise to yield to the drawing of the Spirit!

Have you told your friends about your desire to be right with God? And do they say you are too anxious about these things? Point them to what Christ says about the flames of Gehenna, and ask them if anyone can be too anxious to escape *that!* Point them to what this great old book of God says about the eternal blessedness of Christ's redeemed people, and ask them if anyone can be too anxious to obtain *that!* Speak that solemn word "eternity" to them, and ask them if anyone can be too anxious to escape eternal ruin, and secure eternal well-being! Speak that word "Calvary" to them, and ask them if anyone can be too anxious to possess that great salvation, to bring which to us, the Son of God thought it worthwhile to pay the costly price of His outpoured blood! Soul, seeking salvation, beware of the unwise counsel of well-meaning friends! Our kindest friends can unwittingly be our most dangerous advisers.

## An Individual Concern

Remember that salvation is an *individual* concern. God gave us life one by one, and He deals with us one by one. In the name of Christianity we repudiate those political systems of today which suppress the individual beneath the mass. That rubbishy psychology which treats the nations as so many herds of cattle is a curse to mankind. Those specious, heartless, hireling leaders of modern political mass movements who will make the streets run with human blood to achieve their end, and then huddle men together, in their soul-destroying philosophy of collectivism, treating human beings as a pack of animals to be whipped into obedient servitude, and in which the individual soul is of comparatively no value, are antichristian. Christianity stands for the sacredness and priceless value of the individual. The Good Shepherd, Who gave His life for the sheep, will go out into the desert and among the wild mountains and steep crags to find the one sheep that has strayed. No political system will ever bring that Utopia which the deluded populaces of the world are seeking today. It is not enough simply to change *conditions:* it is *men themselves* that need changing. It does not matter what colour of political shirt a man wears; if the man inside the shirt is not right with God, he will not long be right with his fellow-men. You may make men wear uniform, but that will not make men themselves uniform. Each human personality is unique. Each human soul is of infinite value to God. For each man and woman Christ died on Calvary. The Gospel of Jesus Christ is the only *true* hope of the world; and that Gospel lays all the emphasis on the individual. We call on men and women today to look away from the vain systems of men, to the Lord Jesus Christ. Man-built systems look imposing in their day; but they are paltry in reality, and soon pass away. Let us not be deceived by them. It is still true that *as individuals* we are saved or lost. Unless the second coming of Christ takes place in our lifetime we have each got to die; each to go into eternity, each to stand before God, each to answer, each to receive judgment, each to be saved - or *lost!* O the vital importance, the infinite value, the unspeakable responsibility of the individual! The Lord Jesus stresses this all the way through. We come to Him one by one for salvation. "No man can come to Me except the Father draw him," He says, "and Him that cometh unto Me I will in no wise cast out." O friend, if the gracious Father is drawing you now, let yourself be drawn to the feet of Christ. In *His* eyes you are exceedingly precious, sinful though you be; and He will receive you, will give you the peace of God's forgiveness, will cleanse and heal and save you! No amount of education will save your soul, nor will any political creed. Those of us who boast about our morality know only too well the sin of our hearts. We all *need* salvation. We all need *Jesus Christ*. O receive Him and be saved!

What Must We Do?

How then may we become saved? "I know what you are going to tell us," says someone. "You are going to say that people must become Protestants." Wrong! I am not trying to convert anybody to Protestantism. "But surely you must believe that we are saved either by Protestantism or by Roman Catholicism." No, I do not believe that at all. I do not believe that either of these two systems, as such, can save a single soul. I am not asking any Roman Catholic to turn Protestant. Protestantism, as such, has no more power to save a soul than Roman Catholicism. I am not asking any Anglican to become a Nonconformist, nor any Nonconformist to become an Anglican. I am not asking anybody to become a Baptist, or a Methodist, or a denominationalist of any kind. Protestantism, the Roman Catholic Church, the Church of England, the Nonconformist denominations, are all equally unable, in themselves, to save a single soul. "Well!" exclaims somebody, "I am amazed. I always thought that you preachers taught that a person *must* become a member of *some* church to be saved." No! However many people there are who think that joining a church is necessary for salvation, they are wrong. No church can save. It is Jesus Christ Himself, and Jesus Christ alone, Who is the Saviour of human souls. Am I sure of this? Yes, I am quite sure. This is what the word of God says, "Neither is there salvation in any other: for there is none other name under heaven given among men, whereby we must be saved." Mark that emphatic word - "none other name under heaven" - not Protestantism, the Roman Catholic Church, the Anglican Church, or any other Church, or any other name. Salvation is solely and wholly in Jesus Christ Himself. "What must

I do to be saved?" Here is God's answer: "BELIEVE ON THE LORD
JESUS CHRIST, AND THOU SHALT BE SAVED."

None other Lamb, none other name,
None other hope in heaven or earth or sea;
None other hiding-place from guilt and shame,
None beside Thee.

Simply Believe!

See how *easy* God has made the way of salvation - "Believe on the
Lord Jesus Christ and thou shalt be saved"! Nothing could be plainer
or easier. None of those who perish will ever be able to allege that
the way of salvation was not simple or easy enough. Faith is the
primary and most elementary law of our nature. The first thing a
babe does is to trust. The human babe is the most helpless of all the
new-born. It can do nothing but trust others. Faith is also the *last*
thing with us. When age comes on, and our powers decline, and the
feebleness of a spent and decrepit body leaves us unable to fend for
ourselves, we must trust ourselves to others. Faith is a necessity,
and is natural to us. God has graciously ordered that the necessities
of life are very simple matters for us. We must eat; and even a blind
man can find the way to his mouth. We must drink; and even a babe
knows how to do this without any teaching. Faith is really just as
simple and natural to us. God simply asks us to exercise toward
Him that which we naturally exercise toward others. Trust of oneself
to another is not a "problem" to the babe; nor is it any matter of
peculiar and aggravating intricacy to the aged. Yet when we tell
men that the salvation of the soul comes simply by trusting Christ,
they begin to think this thing and the other about it until presently
they make faith a most perplexing matter. What foolishness is this!
Saving faith is just to take God at His word: simply to rest on the
finished work of Christ. Why need we try to *explain* faith? Our
very endeavours to explain it often becloud it rather than clarify it.
The fact is, all human beings know quite well what it is to believe,
or trust. No explainings are needed.

Are you seeking to be right with God, to be a saved soul, to be sure of forgiveness, to be set free from sin? Away then with all hindering suspicions that there is something mysterious or complicated about faith. Simply and naturally take God at His word. Simply and solely rest upon the finished work of Christ. Do not fall into the snare of looking for some strange new feeling to come over you. Look to Christ alone.

O how unlike the complex works of men,
Heaven's easy, artless, unencumbered plan!
No meretricious graces to beguile,
No clustering ornaments to clog the pile;
From ostentation as from weakness free,
It stands like the cerulean arch we see,
Majestic in its own simplicity.
Inscribed above the portal from afar
Conspicuous as the brightness of a star,
Legible only by the light they give,
Stand the soul-quickening *words - Believe* and *live!*

# THOMAS DEWITT TALMAGE

☙

Thomas Dewitt Talmage (1832-1902). If Charles Spurgeon was the 'Prince of Preachers' then Thomas Dewitt Talmage must be recognised as one of the princes of the American pulpit. Spurgeon said of Talmage's ministry, 'His sermons take hold of my innermost soul. The Lord is with this mighty man. I am astonished when God blesses me, but not when he blesses him.'

From 1856 until 1869 he served as pastor in three Reformed churches and in 1870 his congregation erected the Brooklyn Tabernacle and for 25 years he filled the five thousand seats of that huge auditorium.

He was the founding editor of The Christian Herald; his sermons appeared in three thousand newspapers and magazines a week and he is said to have had twenty-five million readers.

Five hundred of his sermons were published in a twelve volume set.

# Chapter Eight

# THE ALL-DECISIVE STEP

∞

*Believe on the Lord Jesus Christ, and thou shalt be saved.*
- Acts 16:31

∞

Jails are dark, dull, damp, loathsome places even now: but they were worse in the apostolic times. I imagine, today, we are standing in the Philippian dungeon. Do you not feel the chill? Do you not hear the groan of those incarcerated ones who for ten years have not seen the sunlight, and the deep sigh of women who remember their father's house, and mourn over their wasted estates? Listen again. It is the cough of a consumptive, or the struggle of one in the nightmare of a great horror. You listen again, and hear a culprit, his chains rattling as he rolls over in his dreams, and you say: "God pity the prisoner." But there is another sound in that prison. It is a song of joy and gladness. What a place to sing in! The music comes winding through the corridors of the prison, and in all the dark wards the whisper is heard: "What's that? What's that?" It is the song of Paul and Silas. They cannot sleep. They have been whipped, very badly whipped. The long gashes on their backs are bleeding yet. They lie flat on the cold ground, their feet fast in wooden sockets, and of course they cannot sleep. But they can sing. Jailor, what are you doing, with these people? Why have they been put in here? O, they have been trying to make the world better. Is that all? That is all. A pit for Joseph. A lion's cave for Daniel. A blazing furnace for Shadrach. Clubs for John Wesley. An anathema for Philip Melancthon. A dungeon for Paul and Silas. But while we are standing in the gloom of that Philippian dungeon, and we hear the mingling voices of sob, and groan, and blasphemy, and halleujah, suddenly an earthquake! The iron bars of the prison twist, the pillars crack off, the solid masonry begins to heave and rock till the doors swing open, and the walls fall with a terrific crash. The jailor, feeling himself responsible for these prisoners, and feeling suicide to be honourable - since Brutus killed himself, and Cato killed himself, and Cassius killed himself - puts his sword to his own heart, proposing with one strong, keen thrust to put an end to his excitement and agitation. But Paul cries out: "Stop! stop! Do thyself no harm. We are all here." Then I see the jailor running through the dust and amid the ruin of that prison, and I see him throwing himself down at the feet of these prisoners, crying out: "What shall I do? What shall I do?" Did Paul answer: Get out of this place before there is another earthquake put handcuffs and hopples on these other prisoners, lest they get away?" No word of that kind. Compact, thrilling, *tremendous answer;* answer memorable all through earth and heaven. "Believe on the Lord Jesus Christ and thou shalt be saved."

Well, we have all read of the earthquake in Lisbon, in Lima, in Aleppo, and in Caracas; but we live in a latitude where in all our memory there has not been one severe volcanic disturbance. And yet we have seen fifty earthquakes. Here is a man who has been building up a large fortune. His bid on the money market was felt in all the cities. He thinks he has got beyond all annoying rivalries in trade, and he says to himself: "Now I am free and safe from all possible perturbation." But in 1837, or in 1857, or in 1873, a national panic strikes the foundations of the commercial world, and crash! goes all that magnificent business establishment. He is a man who has built up a very beautiful home. His daughters have just come home from the seminary with diplomas of graduation. His sons have started in life, honest, temperate, and pure. When the evening lights are struck, there is a happy and an unbroken family circle. But there has been an accident down at long Branch. The young man ventured too far out in the surf. The telegraph hurled the terror up to the city. An earthquake struck under the foundations of that beautiful home. The piano closed; the curtain dropped; the laughter hushed. Crash! go all those domestic hopes, and prospects, and expectations. So, my friends, we have all felt the shaking down of some great trouble, and there was a time when we were as much excited as this Man of the text, and we cried out as he did: "What shall I do? What shall I do?" The same reply that the Apostle made to him is appropriate to us: "Believe on the Lord Jesus Christ, and thou shalt be saved." The Saviour in some parts of the Bible is called "Lord," and in other parts of the Bible He is called "Jesus," and in other parts of the Bible He is called Christ"; in this passage, all three names come in together - "the Lord Jesus Christ." Now, who is this Being that you want me to trust in and believe in? Men sometimes come to me with credentials and certificates of good character; but I cannot trust them. There is *some dishonesty in their looks* that makes me know I shall be cheated if I confide in them. You cannot put your hearts confidence in a man until you know what stuff he is made of, and am I unreasonable this morning when I stop to ask you who this is that you want me to trust in? No man would think of venturing his life on a vessel going out to sea, that had never been inspected. No, you must have the certificate hung amidships, telling how many tons it carries, and how long ago it was built, and who built it, and all about it. And you cannot expect me to risk the cargo of my immortal interests on board any craft till you tell me what it is made of, and where it was made, and what it is. When, then, I ask you who this is you want me to trust in, you tell me He was a very attractive person. You tell me that the contemporary writers describe Him, and they give the colour of His eyes, and the colour of His hair, and they describe His whole appearance as being resplendent. Christ did not tell the children to come to Him. "Suffer little children to come unto me," was not spoken to the children; it was spoken to the disciples. The children had come without any invitation. No sooner did Jesus appear than the little ones pitched from their mothers' arms, an avalanche of beauty and love, into His lap. "Suffer little children to come unto me." That was addressed to the disciples; not to the children. Christ did not ask John to put his head down on His bosom; John could not help but put his head there. Such eyes, such checks, such a chin, such hair, such physical condition and appearance, why, it must have been completely captivating and winsome. I suppose a look at Him was just to love Him. O! how attractive His manner. Why, when they saw Christ coming along the street, they ran into their houses, and they wrapped up their invalids as quick as they could, and brought them out that He might look at them. O! there was something so pleasant, so inviting, so cheering in everything He did, in His very look. When these sick ones were brought out did He say: "Take away these sores; do not trouble me with these leprosies?" No, no; there was a kind look, there was a gentle word, there was a healing-touch. They could not keep away from Him.

In addition to this softness of character, there was a fiery momentum. How the old hypocrites trembled before Him. How the kings of the earth turned pale. Here is a plain man with a few sailors at His back, coming off the Sea of Galilee, going up to the palace of the Caesars, making that palace quake to the foundations, and uttering a word of mercy and kindness which throbs through all the earth, and through all the heavens, and through all the ages. *O He was a loving Christ.* But it was not effeminacy, or insipidity of character; it was accompanied with majesty, infinite and Omnipotent. Lest the world should not realize His earnestness, this Christ mounts the cross. You say: 'If Christ has to die, why not let Him take some deadly potion and lie on a couch in some bright and beautiful home. If He must die, let Him expire amid all kindly attentions.' No, the world must hear the hammers on the heads of the spikes. The world must listen to the death-rattle of the sufferer. The world must feel His warm blood dropping on each cheek, while it looks up into the face of His anguish. And so the cross must be lifted, and the hole is dug on the top of Calvary. It must be dug three feet deep, and then the cross is laid on the ground, and the sufferer is stretched upon it, and the nails are pounded through nerve, and muscle, and bone, through the right hand, through the left hand; and then they shake His right hand to see if it is fast, and they shake His left foot to see if it is fast, and then they heave up the wood, half a dozen shoulders under the weight, and they put the end of the cross to the mouth of the hole, and they plunge it in, all the weight of His body coming down for the first time on the spikes; and while some hold the cross upright, others throw in the dirt and trample it down, and trample it hard. O, plant that tree well and thoroughly, for it is to bear fruit such as, no other tree ever bore. Why did Christ endure it? He could have taken those rocks, and with them crushed His crucifers. He could have reached up and grasped the sword of the Omnipotent God, and with one clean cut have tumbled them into perdition. But no; He was to die, He must die. His life for my life. His life for your life. In one of the European cities a young man died on the scaffold for the crime of murder. Some time after, the mother of this young man was dying, and the priest came in, and she made confession to the priest that she was the murderer, and not her son in a moment of anger she had struck her husband a blow that slew him. The son came suddenly into the room, and was washing away the wounds and trying to resuscitate his father, when someone looked through the window and, saw him, and supposed him to be the criminal. That young man *died for his own mother.* You say: "It was wonderful that he never exposed her." But I tell you of a grander, thing. Christ, the Son of God, died not for His mother, not for His father, but for His sworn enemies. O, such a Christ as that - so loving, so self-sacrificing - can you not trust Him?

I think there are many under the Spirit of God who are saying: "I will trust Him if you will only tell me how;" and the great question asked by thousands in this assemblage is: "How? how?" And while I answer your question I look up and utter the prayer which Rowland Hill so often uttered in the midst of his sermons: "Master, help!" How are you to trust in Christ? Just as you trust any one. You trust your partner in business with important things. If a commercial house give you a note payable three months hence, you expect the payment of that note at the end of three months. You have perfect confidence in their word and in their ability. You go home today. You expect there will be food on the table. You have confidence in that. Now, I ask you to have the same confidence in the Lord Jesus Christ. He says: "You believe, I take away your sins;" and they are all taken away. "What!" you say: "before I pray any more? before I read my Bible any more? before I cry over my sins any more?" Yes, this moment. Believe with all your heart, and you are saved. Why, Christ is only waiting to get from you what you give to scores of people every day. What is that? Confidence. If these people whom you trust day by day are more worthy than Christ, if they are more faithful than Christ, if they have done more than Christ ever did, then give them the preference; but if you really think that Christ is as trustworthy as they are, then deal with Him as fairly. "O," says some one in a light way: "I believe that Christ was born in Bethlehem, and I believe that He died on the cross." Do you believe it with your head or your heart? I will illustrate the difference. You are in your own house. In the morning you open a newspaper, and you read how Captain Braveheart on the sea risked his life for the salvation of his passengers. You say: "What a grand fellow he must have been! His family deserves very well of the country." You fold the newspaper and sit down at the table, and perhaps do not think of that incident again. That is historical faith. But now you are on the sea, and it is night, and you are asleep, and are awakened by the shriek of "Fire!" You rush out on the deck. You hear, amid the wringing of the hands and the fainting, the cry "No hope! *We are lost!* We are lost!"

The sail puts out its wing of fire, the ropes make a burning ladder in the night heavens, the spirit of wreck hisses in the wave, and on the hurricane-deck shakes out its banner of smoke and darkness. "Down with the life-boats!" cries the captain. "Down with the life-boats!" People rush into them. The boats are about full. Room only for one more man. You are standing on the deck beside the captain. Who shall it be? You or the captain? The captain says: "You," You jump, and are saved. He stands there, and dies. Now, you believe that Captain Braveheart sacrificed himself for his passengers, but you believe it with love, with tears, with hot and long-continued exclamations ; with grief at his loss, and with joy at your deliverance. That is saving, faith. In other words, what you believe with all your heart, and believe in regard to yourself. On this hinge turns my sermon; aye, the salvation of your immortal soul. You often go across a bridge, you know nothing about. You do not know who built the bridge, you do not know what material it is made of; but you come to it, and walk over it, and ask no questions. And here is an arched bridge blasted from the "Rock of Ages," and built by the Architect of the whole Universe, spanning the dark gulf between sin and righteousness, and all God asks you is to walk across it ; and you start, and you come to it, and you stop, and you go a little way on and you stop, and you fall back and you experiment. You say: "How do I know that bridge will hold me?" instead of marching on with firm step, asking no questions, but feeling that the strength of the eternal God is under you. O, was there ever a prize offered so cheap as pardon and heaven are offered to you? For how much? A million dollars? It is certainly worth more than that. But cheaper than that you can have it. Ten thousand dollars? Less than that. Five thousand dollars? Less than that. One dollar? Less than that. One farthing? Less than that. "Without money and without price." No money to pay. No journey to take. No penance to suffer. Only just one decisive action of the soul: "Believe on the Lord Jesus Christ, and thou shalt be saved." Shall I try to tell you what it is to be saved?

*I Cannot tell you.* No man, no angel can tell you. But I can hint at it. For my text brings me up to this point, "Thou shalt be saved." It means a happy life here, and a peaceful death and a blissful eternity. It is a grand thing to go to sleep at night, and to get up in the morning, and to do business all day feeling that all is right between my heart and God. No accident, no sickness, no persecution, no peril, no sword can do me any permanent damage. I am a forgiven child of God and He is bound to see me through. He has sworn He will see me through. The mountains may depart, the earth may burn, the light of the stars may be blown out by the blast of the judgment hurricane; but life and death, things present and things to come are mine. Yea, farther than that - it means a peaceful death.

Mrs. Hemans, Mrs. Sigourney, Dr. Young, and almost all the poets have said handsome things about death. There is nothing beautiful about it. When we stand by the white and rigid features of those whom we love, and they give no answering pressure of the hand, and no returning kiss of the lip, we do not want anybody poetizing around about us. Death is loathsomeness, and midnight, and the wringing of the heart until the tendrils snap and curl in the torture unless Christ be with us. I confess to you to an infinite fear, a consuming horror of death unless Christ shall be with me. I would rather go down into a cave of wild beast or a jungle of reptiles than into the grave unless Christ goes with me. Will you tell me that I am to be carried out from my bright home, and put away in the darkness? I cannot bear darkness. At the first coming of the evening I must have the gas light, and the farther on in life I get, the more I like to have my friends around about me. And am I to be put off for thousands of years in a dark place, with no one to speak to? When the holidays come, and the gifts are distributed, shall I add no joy to the "Merry Christmas," or the "Happy New Year?" Ah, do not point down to the hole in the ground, the grave, and call it a beautiful place; unless there be some supernatural illumination, I shudder back from it. My whole nature revolts at it. But now this, glorious lamp is lifted above the grave, and all the darkness is gone, and the way is clear. I look into it now without a single shudder. Now my anxiety is not about death; my anxiety is that I may live aright; for I know that if my life is consistent when I come to the last hour, and this voice is silent, and these eyes are closed, and these hands with which I beg for your eternal salvation today are folded over the still heart, that then *I shall only begin to live.* What power is there in anything to chill me in the last hour if Christ wraps around me the skirt of His own garment? What darkness can fall upon my eyelids then, amid the heavenly daybreak? O death, I will not fear thee then. Back to thy cavern of darkness thou robber of all the earth. Fly, thou despoiler of families. With this battle-axe I hew thee in twain from helmet to sandal, the voice of Christ sounding all over the earth and through the heavens: "O death I will be thy plague. O grave, I will be thy destruction."

To be saved is to wake up in the presence of Christ. You know when Jesus was upon earth, how happy He made every house He went into, and when He brings us up to His house how great our glee. His voice has more music in it than is to be heard in all the oratories of eternity. Talk not about banks dashed with efflorescence. Jesus is the chief bloom of heaven. We shall see the very face that beamed sympathy in Bethany, and take the very hand that dropped its blood from the short beam of the cross. O, I want, to stand in eternity with Him. Toward that harbour I steer. Toward that goal I run. I shall be satisfied when I awake in His likeness. O, broken-hearted men and women, how sweet it will be in that good land to pour all your hardships, and bereavements, and losses into the loving ear of Christ, and then have Him explain why it was best for you to be sick, and why it was best for you to be widowed, and why it was best for you to be persecuted, and why it was best for you to be tried, and have Him point to an elevation proportionate to your disquietude here, saying: "You suffered with Me on earth, come up now and be glorified with Me in heaven."

Someone went into a house where there had been a good deal of trouble, and said to the woman there : "You seem to be lonely." "Yes," she said, "I am lonely." "How many in the family?" "Only myself." "Have you had any children?" "I had seven children." "Where are they?" "Gone." "All gone? " "All." "All dead?" "All." Then she breathed a long sigh into the loneliness, and said: "O, sir, I have been a good mother to the grave." And so there are hearts here that are utterly broken down by the bereavements of life. I point you today to the eternal balm of heaven. Are there any here that I am missing this morning? O, you poor waiting-maid! your heart's sorrow poured in no human ear, lonely and sad! how glad you will be when Christ shall disband all your sorrows, and crown you queen unto God and the Lamb for ever! O, aged men and women, fed by His love and warmed by His grace for three-score years and ten! will not your decrepitude change for the leap of a heart when you come to look face to face upon Him whom, having not seen, you love? O, that will be the Good Shepherd, not out in the night and watching to keep off the wolves, but with the lambs reclining on the sunlit hill. That will be the Captain of our salvation, not amid the roar, and crash, and boom of battle, but amid His disbanded troops keeping victorious festivity. That will be the Bridegroom of the Church coming from afar, the bride leaning upon His arm while He looks down into her face and says: "Behold, thou art fair my love! Behold thou art fair!"

# CHARLES HADDON SPURGEON

⚭

Charles Haddon Spurgeon is undoubtedly the most famous Baptist minister of the nineteenth century. Converted in 1850, he preached his first sermon at the age of sixteen. When he was eighteen he was invited to become the pastor of the Baptist congregation at Waterbeach, Cambridgeshire. Two years later, he was called to the New Park Street Church in London and within a year of his ministry the church was filled to overflowing. By the time he was twenty-two years of age he was London's most popular preacher, and in order to facilitate the vast crowds who flocked to hear him preach, a much larger building, the Metropolitan Tabernacle, was built in 1861. It seated six thousand, and until his death in 1892, was consistently filled.

During the construction of the Tabernacle, Spurgeon preached to crowds of ten thousand in the Surrey Gardens Music Hall, and on one occasion, at the youthful age of twenty three, he preached to twenty four thousand in the Crystal Palace.

In 1855, he began to publish his sermons every Thursday, at the price of one penny, and today they make up the fifty seven volumes of The Metropolitan Tabernacle Pulpit. This sermon was delivered by Spurgeon at the Metropolitan Tabernacle, on the morning of January 8th 1860.

# Chapter Nine

# THE KING'S HIGHWAY OPENED AND CLEARED

∾

*And they said, Believe on the Lord Jesus Christ,*
*and thou shalt be saved and thy house.*
- Acts 16:31

∾

You will remember that when the children of Israel were settled in Canaan, God ordained that they should set apart certain cities to be called the Cities of Refuge, that to these the man-slayer might flee for security.  If he killed another unawares, and had no malice aforethought, he might flee at once to the City of Refuge; and if he could enter its gates before the avenger of blood should overtake him, he would be secure.  We are told by the rabbis that once in the year, or oftener, the magistrates of the district were accustomed to survey the high roads which led to these cities: they carefully gathered up all the stones, and took the greatest possible precautions that there should be no stumbling-blocks in the way which might cause the poor fugitives to fall, or might by any means impede him in his hasty course.  We hear, moreover, and we believe the tradition to be grounded in fact, that all along the road there were band-posts with the words "Refuge" written very legibly upon them; so that when the fugitive came to a cross-road, he might not need to question for a single moment which was the way of escape; but seeing the well-known word "Refuge," he kept on his breathless and headlong course until he had entered the suburb of the City of Refuge, and he was then at once completely safe.

Now, my brothers and sisters, God has prepared for the sons of men a City of Refuge, and the way to it is by FAITH IN CHRIST JESUS. It is needful, however, that very often the ministers of Christ should survey this road, lest there should be any stumbling-blocks in the path of the poor sinner. I propose this morning to go along it, and, by God's grace, to remove any impediment which Satan may have laid upon the path; and may God so help me, that this survey may be of spiritual benefit to all your souls, that any of you who have been made to stumble in the path of faith, may now pluck up courage, and run joyfully forward, hoping yet to escape from the fierce avenger of your sins.

Well may the minister be careful to keep the road of faith clear for the seeking sinner; for surely the sinner hath a heavy heart to carry, and we ought to make the road as clear and as smooth as we can. We should make straight paths for the feet of these poor benighted souls. It should be our endeavour to cast loads of promises into every slough that runs across the path, that so it may be a king's highway, and may be safe and easy for travelling for those weary feet that have to carry such a heavy heart. Besides, we must remember that the sinner - will make stumbling-blocks enough for himself, even with our greatest and most scrupulous care to remove any others that may naturally lie in his way. For this is one of the sad follies of the poor desponding soul - that it spoils its own road. You have sometimes seen, perhaps, the newly invented engine in the streets, the locomotive that lays down its own pathway and then picks it up again. Now, the sinner is the very reverse of that; he spoils his own road before himself and then carries behind him all the mire and dirt of his own mishaps. Poor soul! he flings stones before himself, cuts out valleys, and casts up mountains in his own pathway. Well may the ministers, then, be careful to keep this road clear. And, let me add, there is another weighty reason. Behind him comes the furious avenger of blood. Oh, how swift is he! There is Moses armed with all the wrath of God, and Death following hard after him - a mounted rider upon his pale horse; and after Death there cometh Hell with all the powers and legions of Satan, and all athirst for blood and swift to slay. Make straight the road, O ministers of Christ, level the mountains, fill up the valleys; for this is a desperate flight, this flight of the sinner from his ferocious enemies towards the one City of Refuge - the atonement of Jesus Christ.

I have thus given the reasons why I am compelled in spirit to make this survey this morning. Come, O Spirit, the Comforter, and help us now, that every stone may be cast out of the high road to heaven.

The road to heaven, my brethren, is BY FAITH IN CHRIST JESUS. It is not by well-doing that you can be saved, though it is by ill-doing, that you will be damned if you put not trust in Christ. Nothing that you can do can save you. Albeit that after you are saved it will be your delightful privilege to walk in the ways of God and to keep His commandments, yet all your own attempts to keep the commandments previous to faith will but sink you deeper into the mire, and will by no means contribute to your salvation. The one road to heaven is BY FAITH IN CHRIST. Or to make it plainer still, as the countryman said, there are but two steps to heaven - out of self into Christ; and, then, out of Christ into heaven. Faith is simply explained as *trusting in Christ*. I find that Christ commands, me to believe in Him, or - to trust Him. I feel that there is no reason in myself why I should be allowed to trust Him. But He commands me to do so. Therefore, altogether apart from my character or from any preparation that I feel in myself, I obey the command, and sink or swim, I trust Christ. Now, that is faith; - when with the eye shut as to all evidence of hope in ourselves, we take a leap in the dark right into the arms of an Omnipotent Redeemer. Faith is sometimes spoken of in Scripture as being a leaning upon Christ; a casting of one's self upon Him; or as the old Puritans used to put it (using a somewhat hard word), it is recumbency on Christ - the leaning of the whole weight upon His cross; ceasing to stand by the strength of one's own power, and resting wholly upon the Rock of ages. The leaving of the soul in the hands of Jesus is the very essence of faith. Faith is receiving Christ into our emptiness. There is Christ, like the conduit in the marketplace. As the water flows from the pipes, so does grace continually flow from Him. By faith I bring my empty pitcher and hold it where the water flows, and receive of its fulness, grace for grace. It is not the beauty of my pitcher. It is not even its cleanness that quenches my thirst: it is simply holding that pitcher to the place where water flows. Even so I am but the vessel, and my faith is the hand which presents the empty vessel to the flowing stream. It is the grace, and not the qualification of the receiver, which saves the soul. And though I hold that pitcher with a trembling hand, and much of that which I seek may be lost through my weakness, yet if the soul be but held to the fountain, and so much as a single drop trickle into it, my soul is saved. Faith is receiving Christ with the understanding and with the will, submitting everything to him, taking him to be my all in all, and agreeing to be henceforth nothing at all. Faith is ceasing from the creature and coming to the Creator. It is looking out of self to Christ, turning the eye entirely from any good thing that is here within me, and looking for every blessing to those open veins, to that poor bleeding heart, to that thorn-crowned head of Him whom God forth set forth "to be the propitiation for our sins, and not for our sins only, but for the sins of the whole world."

Well, having thus described the way, I now come to my real business of removing these stones.

1. A very common impediment in the pathway of the soul that is desiring to be saved, is the *recollection of its past life.* "Oh," saith the sinner, "I dare not trust Christ, because my past sins have been of an unsually black dye. I have been no common sinner, but I have been one singled out from the herd, a very monster in sin. I have taken the highest degree in the devil's college, and have become a master of Belial. I have learned to sit in the seat of the scornful, and have taught others to rebel against God." Ah, soul, I know very well what this impediment is, for once it laid in my way, and very sorely did it trouble me. Before I thought upon my soul's salvation, I dreamed that my sins were very few. All my sins were dead, as I imagined, and buried in the graveyard of forgetfulness. But that trumpet of conviction which aroused my soul to think of eternal things, sounded a resurrection-note to all my sins, and oh, how they rose up in multitudes more countless than the sands of the sea! Now, I saw that my very thoughts were enough to damn me, that my words

would sink me lower than the lowest hell; and as for my acts of sin they now began to be a stench in my nostrils, so that I could not bear them. I recollect the time when I thought I had rather have been a frog or a toad than have been, made a man: when I reckoned that the most defiled creature, the most loathsome and contemptible, was a better thing than myself; for I had so grossly and grievously sinned against Almighty God. Ah, my brethren, it may be that this morning your old oaths are echoing back from the walls of your memory. You recollect how you have cursed God, and you say, "Can I, dare I trust Him whom I have cursed?"

And your old lusts are now rising before you; midnight sins stare you in the face, and snatches of the lascivious song are being yelled in the ear of your poor convinced conscience. And all your sins as they rise up, cry, "Depart, thou accursed one! Depart! thou hast sinned thyself out of grace! Thou art a condemned one! Depart! There is no hope, there is no mercy for thee!"

Now, permit me in the strength and name of God to remove this stumbling-block out of your way. Sinner, I tell thee that all thy sins, be they never so many, cannot destroy thee if thou dost believe on the Lord Jesus Christ. If now thou castest thyself simply on the merits of Jesus, "Though thy sins be as scarlet, they shall be as wool." *Only believe.* Dare to believe that Christ is able to save them to the uttermost that come unto God by Him. Take Him at His word and trust Him. And thou hast a warrant for doing it, for remember it is written, "The blood of Jesus Christ, his Son, cleanseth us from *all sin.*" Thou art commanded to believe, therefore, be thou never so black a sinner, the command is thy warrant - oh, may, God help thee to obey the command. Now, just as thou art, cast thyself on Christ. It is not the greatness of the sinner that is the difficulty: it is the bitterness of the sinner's heart. If now thou art conscious of the most awful guilt, thy guilt becomes as nothing in the eye of God when once He sees the blood of Christ sprinkled upon thee. I tell thee more, if thy sins were ten thousand times as many as they be, yet the blood of Christ is able to atone for them all. Only dare to believe that. Now, by a venturesome faith, trust thyself in Christ. If thou art the most sick of all the wretches that ever this divine Physician essayed to cure, so much the more glory to Him. When a physician cures a man of some little finger-ache or some little disease, what credit doth he get? But when he heals a man who is all over diseased, who has become but a putrid mass, then there is glory to the physician. And so will there be to Christ when He saveth thee. But to put one block out of the way once for all. Remember, sinner, that all the while thou dost not believe in Christ thou art adding to thy sin this great sin of *not believing, which is the greatest sin in the world.* But if thou obey God in this matter of putting thy trust in Christ, God's own Word is guaranteed that thy faith shall be rewarded, and thou shalt find that thy sins which are many are all forgiven thee. By the side of Saul of Tarsus, and of her out of whom was cast seven devils, shalt thou one day stand. With the thief shalt thou sing of love divine, and with Manasseh shalt thou rejoice in Him who can wash away the foulest crimes. Oh, I pray God there may be someone in this great crowd today who may be saying in his heart, "Sir, you have described me. I do feel that I am the blackest sinner anywhere, but I will risk it, I will put my trust in Christ and Christ alone." Ah, soul, God bless thee; thou art an accepted one. If thou canst do this this morning, I will be God's hostage that He will be true to thee and true to His Son, for never sinner perished yet that dared to trust the precious blood of Christ.

2. Now let me endeavor to upheave and eject another stumbling-block. Many an awakened sinner is troubled because of *the hardness of his heart and the lack of what he thinks to be true penitence.* "Oh," saith he, "I can believe that however great my sins are they can be forgiven, but I do not feel the evil of my sins as I ought:-

"My heart how dreadful hard it is
How heavy here it lies!
Heavy and cold within my breast,
Just like a rock of ice."

"I can't feel," says one; "I cannot weep; I have heard of the repentance of others, but I seem to be just like a stone. My heart is petrified, it will not quake at all the thunders of the law, it will not melt before all the wooings of Christ's love." Ah, poor heart, this is a common stumbling-block in the way of those who are really seeking Christ. But let me ask thee one question. Dost thou read anywhere in the Word of God that those who have hard hearts are not commanded to believe? Because if thou can't find such a passage as that, I will be sorry enough to see it, but then I may excuse thee for saying, "I cannot trust Christ because my heart is hard." Do you not know that the Scripture runs thus? "Whosoever believeth in him shall not perish, but have everlasting life." Now, if thou believest, though thy heart be never so hard, thy believing saves thee; and what is more, thy believing shall yet soften thy heart. If thou canst not feel the need of a Saviour as thou wouldest remember that when thou hast a Saviour thou wilt begin then to find out more and more how great was thy need of Him. Why, I believe that many persons find out their needs by receiving the supply. Have you never walked along the street, and looking in at a shop window have seen an article, and have said, "Why, that is just what I want." How do you know that? Why, you saw the thing, and then you wanted it. And I believe there is many a sinner who when he is hearing about Christ Jesus is led to say, "That is just what I want." Did not he know it before? No - poor soul, not till he saw Christ. I find my sense of need of Christ is ten times more acute now than it was before I found Christ. *I thought* I wanted Him for a good many things then, but now I *know* I want Him for everything. I thought there were some things which I could not do without Him; but now I find that without Him I can do nothing. But you say, "Sir, I must repent before I come to Christ." Find such a passage in the Word if you can. Doth not the Word say? "Him hath God exalted with His right hand to be a Prince and a Saviour, for to give repentance to Israel, and forgiveness of sins." Doth not one of our hymns translate that verse into rhyme and put it thus?

"True belief and true repentance,
Every grace that brings us nigh -
Without money,
Come to Jesus Christ and buy."

Oh, these graces are not of nature's spinning. We cannot make these in the loom of the creature. If you would know your need of Christ, take Him now by faith, and sense and feeling shall follow in the rear. Trust Him now for everything. Dare to trust Him. Hard as your heart is, say, "Just as I am, without a plea, but that Thou commandest me, and bid'st me come, I come to thee!" Thy heart shall be softened by the sight of Christ, and love divine shall so sweetly commend itself to thee, that the heart which terrors could not move shall be dissolved by love.

Do understand me, my dear hearers. I want to preach in the broadest manner I possibly can this morning the doctrine that we are justified by faith alone; that man is commanded to believe; and that altogether apart from anything in man, man has a right to believe. Not from any preparation that he feels, not from anything good he discerns in himself; but he has a right to believe, simply because he is commanded to believe; and if, relying upon the fact that he is commanded, God the Holy Spirit enables him to believe, that faith will surely save the soul, and deliver him from the wrath to come. Let me take up, then, that stumbling stone about hardness of heart. Oh, soul, trust Christ and thy heart shall be softened. And may God the Holy Spirit enable thee to trust Him, hard heart and all, and then thy hard heart shall soon be turned into a heart of flesh, and thou shalt love Him who hath loved thee.

3. Now, for a third stumbling-block. "Oh," saith some poor soul, "I do not know whether I believe or not, sir. Sometimes I do believe; but oh, *it is such little faith* I have that I cannot think Christ can save me." Ah, there you are again you see, looking to yourself. This has made many trip and fall. I pray God I may put this out of your way. Poor sinner, remember it is not the *strength* of thy faith that saves thee, but the *reality* of thy faith. What is more, it is not even the reality of thy faith that saves thee, it is the object of thy faith. If thy faith be fixed on Christ, though it seems to be in itself a line no thicker than a spider's cobweb, it will hold thy soul throughout time and eternity. For remember it is not the thickness of this cable of faith, it is the strength of the anchor which imparts strength to the cable, and so shall hold thy ship in the midst of the most fearful storm. The faith that saves man is sometimes so small that the man himself cannot see it. A grain of mustard seed is the smallest of all seeds, and yet if thou hast but that quantity of faith, thou art a saved man. Remember what the poor woman did. She did not come and take hold of Christ's person with her hand, she did not throw her

arms about his knees; but she stretched out her finger, and then - she did not touch Christ's feet or even His dress - she touched but the ravelling, the fringe of His garment, and she was made whole. If thy faith be but as little as that, seek to get more of it, but still remember that it will save thee. Jesus Christ himself compares Little-faith to a smoking flax. Does it burn? is there any fire at all! No; there is nothing but a little smoke, and that is most offensive. "Yes," saith Jesus, "but I will not quench it." Again, he compares it to a bruised reed. Of what service is it? It is broken; you cannot bring music from it; it is but a reed when it is whole, and now it is a bruised reed. Break it, snap it, throw it away? "No," says He. "I will not break the bruised reed." Now, if that is the faith thou hast, the faith of the smoking flax, the faith of the bruised reed, thou art saved. Thou wilt have many a trial and many a trouble in going to heaven with so little faith as that, for when there is little wind to a boat there must be much tugging at the oar; but still there will be wind enough to land thee in glory, if thou dost simply trust Christ, be that trust never so feeble. Remember a little child belongs to the human race as much as the greatest giant; and so a babe in grace is as truly a child of God as is Mr. Great-heart, who can fight all the giants on the road. And thou mayest be as much an heir of heaven in thy minority, in the infancy of thy grace, as thou wilt be when thou shalt have expanded into the full grown Christian, and shalt become a perfect man in Christ Jesus. It is not, I tell thee, the *strength of thy faith,* but *the obect* of thy faith. It is the blood, not the hyssop; not the hand that smites the lintel, but the blood that secures the Israelite in the day when God's vengeance passes by. Let that stumbling-block be taken out of the way.

4. "But," saith another, "I do think sometimes I have a little faith, but I *have* so many *doubts and fears.* I am tempted every day to believe that Jesus Christ did not die for me, or that my belief is not genuine, or that I never experienced the regenerating influence of the Holy Spirit. Tell me, sir, can I be a true believer in Christ if I have doubts and fears?" My answer is simply this, there is no Scripture which saith, that "He that believeth shall be damned, if that faith be mixed with doubts." "He that believeth shall be saved,"

be that faith never so little, and even though it be intermingled with multitudes of doubts and fears. You remember that memorable story of our Saviour, when he was on board a ship with His disciples. The winds roared, the ship rocked to and fro, the mast was strained, the sails were rent, and the poor disciples were full of fear - "Lord, save us, or we perish." Here were doubts. What did Jesus say when He rebuked them? "Why are ye fearful" O ye of *no* faith? No; "O ye of little faith." So there may be little faith where there are great doubts. There is light at eventide in the air; even though there is a great deal of darkness, yet there is light. And if thy faith should never come to noonday, if it do but come to twilight, thou art a saved man. Nay, more, if it doth not come to twilight, if thy faith is but starlight, nay, candlelight, nay, a spark - if it be but a glow-worm spark, thou art saved; and all thy doubts, and all thy fears, and thy distresses, terrible though they may be, can never trample thee in the dust, can never destroy thy soul. Do you not know that the best; of God's children are exercised with doubts and fears even to the last? Look at such a man as John Knox. There was a man who could face the frowns of a world, who could speak like a king to kings, and fear no man; yet on his dying bed he was troubled about his interest in Christ. because be was tempted to self-righteousness. If such a man have doubts, dost *thou* expect to live without them? If God's brightest saints are exercised, if Paul himself keeps under his body lest he should be a castaway, why, how canst thou expect to live without clouds? Oh, my dear man, drop the idea that the prevalence of thy doubts disproves the truth of the promise. Again believe; away with all thy doubts; sink or swim, cast thyself on Jesus; and thou canst not be lost, for His honour is engaged to save every soul that puts its trust in Him.

5. "Ah," says another, "but you have not yet hit upon my fear." I used when I first knew the Saviour, to try myself in a certain manner, and often did I throw stumbling-blocks in my path through it, and therefore I can speak very affectionately to any of you who are doing the same. Sometimes I would go up into my chamber, and by way of self-examination, I seek to ask myself this question – *Am I afraid to die?* If I should drop my head down in my chamber, can I say that I should joyfully close my eyes? Well, it often happened that I could

not honestly say so. I used to feel that death would be a very solemn thing. Ah, then I said, "I have never believed in Christ for if I had put my trust in the Lord Jesus, I should not be afraid to die, but I should be quite confident." I do not doubt that there are many here who are saying, "Sir, I cannot follow Christ, because I am afraid to die; I cannot believe that Jesus Christ will save me, because the sight of death makes me tremble." Ah, poor soul, there are many of God's blesssed ones, who through fear of death have been much of their lifetime subject to bondage. I know precious children of God now: I believe that when they die, they will die triumphantly; but I know, this, that the thought of death is never pleasing to them. And this is accounted for, because God has stamped on nature that law, the love of life and self-preservation. And again, the man that hath kindred and friends, it is natural enough that he should scarce like to leave behind those that are so dear. I know that when he gets more grace he will rejoice in the thought of death; but I do know that there are many quite safe, who could die triumphantly, who now, in the prospect of death, feel afraid of it. I remember my aged grandfather once preach a sermon which I have not forgotten. He was preaching from the text "The God of all grace," and he somewhat interested the assembly, after describing the different kinds of grace that God gave, by saying at the end of each period, "But there is one kind of grace that you do not want." After each sentence there came the like, "But there is one kind of grace you do not want." And, then, he wound up by saying, "You don't want dying grace in living moments, but you shall have dying grace when you want it." Now you are testing yourself by a condition in which you are not placed. If you are placed in the condition, you shall have grace enough if you put your trust in Christ. In a party of friends we were discussing the question, whether if the days of martyrdom should come, we were prepared to be burned. Well, now, I must frankly say, that speaking as I feel today, I am not prepared to be burned. But I do believe if there were a stake in Smithfield, and I knew that I were to be burned there at one o'clock, that I should have grace enough to be burned at one o'clock; but I have not yet got to a quarter past twelve, and the time is not come yet. Do not expect dying grace until you want it, and when the time comes, you may be sure you will have sufficient grace to bear it. Cast out that stumbling-block then. Rest thyself on Christ, and trust a living Christ to help thee in thy dying hour.

6. Another most grievous perplexity to many a seeking soul is this: "Oh, I would trust Christ, but *I feel no joy.* I hear the children of God singing sweetly about their privileges, I hear them saying that they have been to the top of Pisgah and have viewed the promised land, have taken a pleasant prospect of the world to come; but oh, my faith yields me no joy. I hope I do believe, but at the same time I have none of those raptures. My worldly troubles press heavily upon me, and sometimes even my spiritual woes are greater than I can bear." Ah, poor soul, let me cast out that stone from thy road. Remember, it is not written, "he that is joyful shall be saved," but "he that *believeth* shall be saved." Thy faith will make thee joyful by-and-by; but it is as powerful to save thee even when it does not make thee rejoice. Why look at many of God's people, how sad and sorrowful they have been! I know they ought not to be. This is their sin; but still it is such a sin that it does not destroy the efficacy of faith. Notwithstanding all the sorrows of the saint, faith still keeps alive, and God is still true to his promise. Remember, it is not what you feel that saves you; it is what you believe. It is not feeling but believing. "We walk by faith, not by sight." When I feel my soul as cold as an iceberg, as hard as a rock, and as sinful as Satan, yet even then faith ceases not to justify. Faith prevails as truly in the midst of sad feelings as of happy feelings, for then, standing alone, it proves the majesty of its might. Believe, O son of God, believe in Him, and look not for aught in thyself.

7. Then, again, there are many that are distressed because *they have blasphemous thoughts.* Here, too, I can heartily sympathize with many. I remember a certain narrow and crooked lane in a certain country town, along which I was walking one day while I was seeking the Saviour. On a sudden the most fearful oaths that any of you can conceive rushed through my heart. I put my hand to my mouth to prevent the utterance. I had not, that I know of, ever heard those words; and I am certain that I had never used in my life from my youth up so much as one of them, for I had never been profane. But

these things sorely beset me; for half an hour together the most fearful imprecations would dash through my brain. Oh, how I groaned and cried before God! That temptation passed away; but ere many days it was renewed again; and when I was in prayer, or when I was reading the Bible, these blasphemous thoughts would pour in upon me more than at any other time. I consulted with an aged godly man about it. He said to me, "Oh, all this many of the people of God have proved before you. But," said he, "do you hate these thoughts?" "I do," I truly said. "Then," said he, "they are not yours; serve them as the old parishes used to do with vagrants - whip them and send them on to their own parish. "So," said he, "do with them. Groan over them, repent of them, and send them on to the devil, the father of them, to whom they belong - for they are not yours." Do you not recollect how John Bunyan hits off the picture? He says, when Christian was going through the Valley of the Shadow of Death, "There stepped up one to him, and whispered blasphemous thoughts into his ear, so that poor Christian thought they were his own thoughts; but they were not his thoughts at all, but the injections of a blasphemous spirit." So when you are about to lay hold on Christ, Satan will ply all his engines and try to destroy you. He cannot bear to lose one of his slaves: he will invent a fresh temptation for each believer so that he may not put his trust in Christ. Now, come, poor soul, notwithstanding all these blasphemous thoughts in thy soul, dare to put thy trust in Christ. Even should those thoughts have been more blasphemous than any thou hast ever heard, come trust in Christ, come cast thyself on Him. I have heard that when an elephant is going over a bridge he will sound the timber with his foot to see if it will bear him over. Come thou who thinkest thyself an elephantine sinner, here is a bridge that is strong enough for thee, even with all these thoughts of thine, "All manner of sin and blasphemy shall be forgiven thee." Throw that in Satan's face and trust thyself in Christ.

8. One other stumbling-block, and I will have done. Some there be that say, "Oh, sir, I would trust in Christ to save me *if I could see that my faith brought forth fruits.* Oh, sir, when I would do good, evil is present with me." Excuse my always bringing in my own

feelings as an illustration, but I feel when I am preaching to tried sinners, that the testimony of one's own experience is generally more powerful than any other illustration that can be found. It is not, believe me, any display of egotism, but the simple desire to come home to you, that makes me state what I have felt myself. The first Sunday after I came to Christ, I went to a Methodist chapel. The sermon was upon this text: "O wretched man that I am! who shall deliver me from the body of this death?" I had just got as far as that in the week. I knew that I had put my trust in Christ, and I knew that, when I sat in that house of prayer, my faith was simply and solely fixed on the atonement of the Redeemer. But I had a weight on my mind, because I could not be as holy as I wanted to be. I could not live without sin. When I rose in the morning I thought I would abstain from every hard word, from every evil thought and look; and I came up to that chapel groaning, because "when I would do good evil was present with me." The minister said that when Paul wrote the verse I have quoted, he was not a Christian; that this was his experience before he knew the Lord. Ah, what error, for I know that Paul was a Christian, and I know the more Christians look to themselves the more they will have to groan, because they cannot be what they want to be. What! - you will not believe in Christ until you are perfect? Then you will never believe in Him. You will not trust the precious Jesus till you have no sins to trust Him with! Then you will never trust Him at all. For rest assured you will never be perfect till you see the face of God in heaven. I knew one man who thought himself a perfect man, and that man was humpbacked. This was my rebuke to his pride, "Surely if the Lord gave you a perfect soul he would give you a perfect body to carry it in." Perfection will not be found this side of the grave. Your business is to trust in Christ. You must depend on nothing but the blood of Christ. Trust in Christ and you stand secure. "He that believeth on the Son of God hath everlasting life." It is our duty to fight against corruption; it is our privilege to conquer it; it is our honour to feel that we are fighting against sin; it shall be our glory one day to tread it beneath our feet. But today expect not complete victory. Your very consciousness of sin proves that you are alive. The very fact that you are not what you want to be proves that there are some high and noble thoughts in you that could not have come by nature. You were content with yourself some six weeks ago, were you not? And the fact that you are discontent now, proves that God has put a new life into you, which makes you seek after a higher and better element in which to breathe. When you become what you want to be on earth, then despair. When the law justifies you, then you have fallen from grace; for Paul has said, "When we are justified by the law, we are fallen from grace." But while I feel that the law condems me, it is my joy to know that believing in Christ, "There is no condemnation to him that is in Christ Jesus, who walks not after the flesh, but after the Spirit."

And now though I have been trying to clear the way, I feel conscious that very likely I have been putting a stone or two in the road myself. May God forgive me - it is a sin of inadvertence. I would lay this road as straight and clear as ever was turnpike road between one city and another. Sinner, there is nothing which can rob thee of *thy right* to believe in Christ. Thou art freely invited to come to the marriage banquet. The table is spread, and the invitation freely given. There are no porters at the door to keep thee out there are none to ask a ticket of admission of thee:-

"Let not conscience make you linger:
Nor of fitness fondly dream;
All the fitness He requireth
Is to feel your need of Him
This He gives you:
'Tis His Spirit's rising beam."

Come to Him just as thou art. But, ah, I know that when we sit in our studies it seems a light thing to preach the gospel and make people believe in Christ; but when we come to practice, it is the hardest thing in the world. If I were to tell you to do some great thing you would do it; but simply, when it is, "Believe, wash, and be clean!" you will not do it. If I said, "Give me ten thousand pounds," you would give it. You would crawl a thousand miles on your hands and knees, or drink the bitterest draught that was ever concocted; but this trusting in Christ is too hard for your proud spirit. Ah, sinner, art thou too proud to be saved? Come, man, I beseech thee for the love of Christ, by the love of thy own soul, come with me, and let us go together to the foot of the cross. Believe on Him who hangs groaning there; oh, put thy trust in Him who is risen from the dead, and has led captivity captive. And if thou trust Him, poor sinner, thou shalt not be disappointed; it shall not be trust misplaced. Again I say it, I am content to be lost if thou art lost trusting in Christ; I will make my bed in hell with thee should God reject thee, if thou puttest thy simple trust in Christ. I dare to say that, and to look *that* boldly in the face; for thou wouldst be the first sinner that was ever cast away trusting in Jesus. "But, oh," saith one, "I cannot think that such a wretch as I am can have a right to believe." Soul, I tell thee it is not whether thou art a wretch, or not a wretch; it is *the command* that is thy warrant. Thou art commanded to believe." And when a command comes home with power, the power comes with the command; and he who is commanded, being made willing, casts himself on Christ, and he believes, and is saved.

I have laboured this morning to try and make myself as clear as I can about this doctrine. I know if any man is saved it is the work of God the Holy Ghost from first to last. "If any man is regenerate, it is not of the will of the flesh, nor of blood, but of God." But I do not see how that great truth interferes with this other, "Whosoever believeth in Christ shall be saved." And I would again, even to the falling down on my knees, as though God did beseech you by me, pray you, "In Christ's stead be ye reconciled to God." And this is the reconciliation, "That ye believe on the Lord Jesus Christ whom he hath sent," that ye trust Christ. Do you understand me? That ye cast yourself on Him; that ye depend on nothing but what He has done. Saved you must be, lost you cannot be, if you fling yourself wholly upon Christ, and cast the whole burden of your sins, your doubts, your fears, and your anxieties wholly there. Now, this is preaching free grace doctrine. And if any wonder how a Calvinist can preach thus, let me say that this is the preaching that Calvin preached, and, better still, it is the preaching of our Lord Jesus Christ and His apostles. We have divine warrant when we tell you, "He that believeth and is baptized shall be saved; he that believeth not shall be damned."

# JOHN LINTON

John Linton was one of twelve children who immigrated with his parents from Scotland to America. Like the prodigal son his early life was steeped in sin, and by the time he was thirteen he had left home and was living rough. But God's grace reached him through the life of a Christian lady who had taken him in and under her godly influence he was won for Christ.

Later he moved to Canada, and at James Street Baptist church, Hamilton Ontario he heard God' s call to become a preacher.

He attended Gordon Bible College in Boston, then Colleges in Woodstock, Toronto and Manitoba, finally graduating with a master's degree.

It was while he was pastoring at High Park Baptist church, Toronto that he became interested in evangelism. Resigning his pastorate to become a full time evangelist, he travelled across Canada and America seeing the blessing of God upon his ministry as he won many converts to Christ.

He died in the pulpit at the age of 77 while conducting an evangelical service.

# Chapter Ten

# HOUSEHOLD SALVATION

∞

*Believe on the Lord Jesus Christ,*
*and thou shalt be saved, and thy house.*
- Acts 16:31

∞

One night in a church in southern Illinois, I began a sermon on this text by saying that recently in a certain church I noticed on the wall behind the pulpit my text quoted in this way - "Believe on the Lord Jesus Christ, and thou shalt be saved." I told the people that was not how the text read in the Bible, that they had left out the last three words, and they were the best part of the text. I said, "I hope, with God's help, to preach such a sermon on these last three glorious words that nobody here will ever misquote that text." Seeing my audience was a little disturbed, I followed their gaze, and there above my head on the wall of that church, also, was the same text with the same omission!

There are some verses in the Bible, which, if they could speak, would have a real complaint to make against the people of God. They are being continually abused and distorted by misquotation. This verse is one of them. When Paul said to the Philippian jailor, "Believe on the Lord Jesus Christ, and thou shalt be saved," he did not stop there. Why do we stop there? Paul did not say that if he believed, one thing would happen. He said two things would happen, and the second was far greater than the first. Why, then, do we emasculate and limit this glorious promise? Why quote only one of the two things Paul mentioned? Why this strange silence concerning those wonderful words, "and thy house"? The text reads, "Believe on the Lord Jesus Christ, and thou shalt be saved, AND THY HOUSE."

These words not only teach that if a man believes God for the salvation of his soul he will be saved, but also, that if he believes God will save his household, God will as surely save his house for his faith, as He saves that man's soul for his faith.

In other words, it is the expressly declared will of God that the whole family of a believer should be saved. And the one condition of their being saved is for that believer to ask and believe that God will save them.

If a man comes to God and asks God to save him, and with a Spirit-given faith believes that God that moment does so, can he go from God's presence knowing of a surety that he is saved? Certainly. Why? Because God says so - "Believe . . . and thou shalt be saved." And if that same man asks God to save his family, and with the same kind of faith, which he had when he believed for his own salvation, he believes God for their salvation (that is, he believes that God in His own good time and in His own wonderful way will save them), can he go on his way knowing of a surety that God will save them? Certainly. Why? Because God says so, "Believe and thy house shall be saved."

This surely is glad news to the children of God. Could there be any more welcome and wonderful news to those with loved ones unsaved than that God pledges His word of honor to hear and answer believing prayer for the household of a Christian? The greatest desire of any Christian parent's heart is to be able to stand before God in Heaven and say, "Behold I and the children God hath given me." This heart's desire is covered in a general way by the promise in Mark 11:24, "What things soever ye desire, when ye pray, believe that ye receive them, and ye shall have them." It is covered, however, in a specific way by the promise in my text - "Believe . . . and thou shalt be saved, AND THY HOUSE."

I did not always see this truth. I thought the text meant this, "Mr. Jailor, if you believe, you will be saved. And since we see you have a family, we would tell you that if they also believe, they, too, will be saved." But that is not what the Bible says. Paul is not talking to the jailor about their faith and what it will do, but about his own faith and what it will do. It was to the jailor Paul said, "Believe and thy house shall be saved."

Someone will say, "But surely God will not save my family unless they believe for themselves." No, of course not. But that has nothing to do with us. That is God's part in this covenant. Our part is to ask God to save them and believe God will do so. God's part is so to move upon them that, convicted of sin, they will see their need as they never saw it, and of their own free will turn to God.

Notice that the text does not say that IF WE PRAY for the salvation of our family they will be saved. It does not say that. It is not prayer for them that will necessarily save them. It is BELIEVING for their salvation that saves them. Only when we prayed believingly for ourselves were we saved, and only when we pray believingly for them, does God promise to save them. Assuredly they will not be saved unless they believe for themselves, but they will believe for themselves and be saved if we believingly ask God to save them and TRUST GOD TO BRING THAT TO PASS.

Let me show you from several different angles that this golden, glorious promise means what I have just said.

## 1 Household Salvation Is in Harmony With the Constitution of Things on Earth

God has set mankind in families. He said, "It is not good that the man should be alone." So He ordained the ordinance of marriage; and God looks on the family as a unit. The children in a family are part of the father and mother; and when parents are saved, it becomes the special desire of God to save their children.

But the promise applies to any member of a household as well as to parents. Children are no more part of their parents, than parents are part of the children. If a son believes God for the salvation of his parents, God will honor his faith and save them. "He shall turn the heart of the fathers to the children, and the heart of the children to their fathers" (Malachi 4:6). That is what happens in every genuine revival. Believing parents begin praying for their unsaved children, and believing children begin praying for their unsaved fathers. Every Christian is a member of a family, so why should it be thought a thing incredible that God gives a promise for the salvation of a family, as well as of an individual? Since God ordained families, He wants to save families.

## 2. Household Salvation Is in Harmony With Things in Heaven

Heaven itself is built on the family principle. God speaks of Heaven above as a home. It is "my Father's house." The Bible describes the church as a family, "The whole family in heaven and earth." His people are called "the household of faith." He Himself is called "our Father . . . in heaven." We are told that Abraham, Isaac and Jacob; father, son, and grandson, shall sit together in the kingdom of Heaven. It is God's stated desire to save the family of a Christian so that the family as a unit shall be together in Heaven. He wants the Christian's home on earth to be a miniature Heaven, and to make this possible, He promises to answer believing prayer and bring this to pass.

Let me ask every Christian parent, and every member of a family - do you believe that this promise given to the Philippian jailor has also been given to you? You will readily grant that the first part is yours - "Believe . . . and thou shalt be saved." You believe that is yours. Now, do you believe the words, "and thy house," are for you, or only for the jailor? The fact is this thrilling promise is for every believer. God wants to save your family with you. "Thou . . . and thy house" is what God says. He has joined us and our household together, and what God hath joined in this wonderful promise, let no man put asunder.

You may say, "This promise is not for me because I have no such wonderful faith as to believe for my entire family." My friend, you have faith or you never could have been saved. The Spirit of God imparted faith to you at your conversion. Let me ask you, where is your faith?  God gave you faith; you put it to work; it saved you. Why do you think God gave us this faith?  Merely to save our own poor little souls?  No, He gave us faith for our own salvation first, and then for the salvation of others, beginning with our household. Therefore, use this faith that saved your own soul to save the souls of others, particularly those of your household.

It is a wonderful thing when God saves a man in response to his faith.  It is a more wonderful thing when God saves a man's family in response to his faith.  When the first part of the text is believed, one soul is saved.  When the second part is believed, a whole household is saved.  No wonder Satan tries to keep us from seeing and believing the whole of this promise.

### 3. Household Salvation Is Taught All Through the Scriptures

It is not in one isolated passage of Scripture that this wonderful truth is taught, or I could never with such confidence preach it.  The Bible is full of it.  The marvel is that this comforting, challenging truth is so little known.

Look at the first gospel invitation in the Bible.  "And the Lord said unto Noah, Come thou and all thy house into the ark" (Genesis 7:1). Right at the beginning of the Bible, God lets it be known that His will is not to save a man alone, but all his house.  What was Noah's response to this offered privilege?  "By faith Noah. . . . prepared an ark to the saving of his house" (Hebrews 11:7).  He believed God would give him his family, including his three daughters-in-law.  As proof of his faith, he prepared an ark, with room for all his family. What was God's response to his faith?  God gave him every member of his family, for eight souls were saved through the flood.  Thus, the first example of family salvation in the Bible included the in-laws, those brought into the family through marriage.

The Passover, in Exodus 12, is a divine illustration of faith for a family.  God saved Israel that night by families.  The father was to "take a lamb for an house."  The father sprinkled the blood on the door, and because of his faith, the whole family was saved.

Rahab, in Joshua 2, is another example of family salvation.  She lived on the wall of the doomed city of Jericho.  When the fall of the city was imminent, she was given a promise of salvation. *But Rahab did not want to be saved alone.* Who wants to be saved alone? If we are content to be saved alone, and are not deeply concerned for the salvation of our loved ones, we need to be saved from selfishness. When Rahab voiced her faith to the two men, she asked not only for her own salvation, but said, "I pray . . . that ye will save alive my father, and my mother, and my brethren, and my sisters, and all that they have." Some of her brothers and sisters were evidently married and had children. She could not think of them all being destroyed in the judgment upon the city, so she pleaded for their salvation, including all that they had. And what did God do about that? What was His response to her believing prayer? Just what it will be to ours today. God gave Rahab just what she went after. "And Joshua saved Rahab . . . alive, and her father's household, AND ALL THAT SHE HAD" (Joshua 6:25).

Consider Joshua himself as he stands before Israel and says, "Choose you this day whom ye will serve . . . but as for me and my house, we will serve the Lord" (Joshua 24:15). Here was a public statement of Joshua's faith that his household would serve God. How did he know they would? He knew it by faith. He is so certain his family will serve God that he is ready to stand before a whole nation in general assembly and proclaim the fact. You may say, "Suppose they had not served God." I reply, "Joshua supposed no such thing. He believed they would." When we really believe God will do a thing, we do not run around supposing the opposite.

Here is where many a dear mother fails to offer believing prayer for her children. She prays and worries, and worries and prays. If she really believed God was going to save her boy, she would pray and praise. She would present her supplication *"with thanksgiving,"* knowing of a surety that God would save her boy. But because she does not really believe this, she prays with worrying. Mother, when you believe you do not worry, and when you worry you do not believe. If you will recognize that it is the will of God that your son be saved, that it is not the will of God that any should perish, and that God is pledged to answer believing prayer; and if you will wait before God in prayer, asking Him to give you faith enough to claim your son's salvation; then God, by His Spirit, will give you the assurance of his salvation, and from that moment you will pray, not with worrying, but with thanksgiving, praising God for the answer before it comes. Through *faith* "women received their dead raised to life again" (Hebrews 11:35). This is true in the spiritual realm, as many a believing mother can testify. Joshua did not worry. He believed God, and God honored Joshua's faith. His family served God.

This same precious truth is found hidden in the arithmetic of the book of Job. In the first chapter, we are told of Job's possessions. They are carefully enumerated: "His substance also was seven thousand sheep, and three thousand camels, and five hundred yoke of oxen, and five hundred she asses." In addition to these we read, "There were born unto him SEVEN SONS AND THREE DAUGHTERS."

There is no word that Job's children honored God in their lives. They may have done so, but Scripture does not record it. They spent much of their time feasting and dancing. But their father prayed for them unceasingly. "And it was so, when the days of their feasting were gone about, that Job sent and sanctified them, and rose up early in the morning, and offered burnt-offerings according to the number of them all: for Job said, It may be that my sons have sinned. . . . Thus did Job continually" (Job 1:5).

The calamity that befell Job swept away all his cattle and his entire family. In that terrible trial, however, Job's faith stood fast; and in the last chapter of the story, God rewarded him by giving him double of all that he had before: "Also the Lord gave Job TWICE AS MUCH as he had before."

Mark now the arithmetic. The thousands and hundreds of each kind of cattle were doubled. "So the Lord blessed the latter end of Job more than his beginning: for he had fourteen thousand sheep, and six thousand camels, and a thousand yoke of oxen, and a thousand she asses. He had also seven sons and three daughters" (Job 42:12-13). Why not fourteen sons and six daughters? God was to give him twice as much. The other possessions were doubled, why not the children?

The explanation is that although the cattle were destroyed forever, Job's children were still alive in the other world; and not only that, but they were in God's care there where their father would one day meet them. Had they gone to the realm of the unsaved dead, Job would never have seen them again. They would have been gone indeed. But he still had them, for they were not lost, only gone before into the abode of the righteous where later he would join them. They were his forever, because he prayed for them continually, and God is faithful in answering such prayer.

Take the case of Cornelius in Acts 10. He was a centurion in the Roman army, a heathen man who had heard of the one true God. He prayed for salvation, and God sent an angel with this message, "Send ... for ... Peter ... he shall tell thee what thou oughtest to do." Why did God include Cornelius' house? Because it was God's desire to save, not this man alone, but all of his family; so the promise included his house. Here we are at the other end of the Bible, and the same truth stares us in the face.

And Cornelius took God at His word. He went out and "called together his kinsmen and near friends." Now the angel of God had said not a word about "near friends," but this man pushed out the bounds of God's promise to include some special friends of his whose salvation he desired, as well as his own and that of his household. And pray, what did God do about that? He honored Cornelius' faith; and while Peter was preaching, "the Holy Ghost fell on *all them which heard the word.*" The same God who gave Noah his daughters-in-law, who gave Rahab all she had prayed for, here gives Cornelius not only his family, but also the friends whom his faith and compassion embraced.

And so from beginning to end of the Bible we see that it is God's express desire to save the whole family of a believer. Not only to the Philippian jailor, but to others in Bible history, and to us today does God say, "Believe . . . and thou shalt be saved, and thy house."

## 4. Household Salvation Has Marked the Dealings of God With Men All Through History

Since the canon of Scripture closed, God has been honoring the faith of men and women for the saving of their house.

When a Christian mother in the fifth century went to the Bishop of Milan and implored him with tears to speak to her profligate son, the Bishop marked her tears, and with prophetic insight said, "It is impossible that the child of such prayers could ever be lost." That mother was Monica, and her son the saintly Augustine, converted to God by the faith of a mother who would not let God go. She gave God no rest, day or night, until her boy was saved.

Catherine Booth is reported to have prayed, "O God, I will not stand before Thee without all my children." She was actually not willing to be saved without them. What was God's answer to such passionate pleading and faith? Every one of them was saved and became a preacher of the gospel.

Jonathan Edwards in a moment of intimacy with God is said to have claimed from God that - not one of his seed would ever be lost! After three generations, one who had made investigation could not find one of his descendents who was not a decided Christian.

In the winter of 1909, I attended the Gordon Bible School in Boston. It was founded by Dr. A. J. Gordon. Mrs. Gordon, his widow, was one of our teachers. She impressed upon us the fact that God had given every parent the privilege of claiming his children for God. She said if a parent would plead and *believe* God's promise, the child of such faith would never be lost. God had given her five children. From their birth she claimed and believed God for their salvation. As the children grew up, they one by one accepted Christ. Ernest Gordon who writes so ably for the *Sunday School Times* was the fruit of such praying. It is faith like this that God honors.

The first time I preached this sermon, a Christian mother in my church in Toronto was convicted of the sin of unbelief. She had three grown-up children. One was a backslidden Christian, a girl of eighteen, worldly and uninterested in spiritual things. Two sons were unsaved. This mother prayed and worried, which means that she did not believe God would answer her prayers. She saw the meaning of Acts 16:31. She began to pray with faith. She herself became a different woman. Instead of fretting over her children, she became filled with joy and peace through believing. In a few weeks her daughter was beautifully restored to fellowship with God.

She became an earnest soul-winning Christian. A week or two later, the younger of the two boys was converted and later went to Bible college. About a year later the older son was saved, so that the whole family was united in Christ. This widowed mother then began praying for her married sister and her family who lived fifteen miles from Toronto. One by one they accepted Christ, and I received them into the church. Nine members of those two families accepted Christ because a mother took God at His word and believed for her house.

I preached this sermon in the First Baptist Church, New York, shortly after noble Dr. Haldeman had gone in to see the King. At the close of the service a lady told me that three years before, in a public meeting in that church, a man rose under the gallery and gave a ringing testimony for Christ. He closed by saying, "Five years ago a dying mother called her daughter to her bedside and told her how glad she was that all her children would be with her in Heaven. The daughter said, "Why, mother, what about John?" The dying mother then quoted the words, "Believe . . . and thou shalt be saved, and thy house." The man said, "I am that son, picked up from the gutter by a God who answers prayer."

The Rev. Christian Eicher heard me preach this message in the Grand Opera House in Chicago. After the service, he told me this story: His father was converted in middle life. He saw the meaning of Acts 16:31. He claimed his household for God. He had twelve children, none of whom was saved. Five were then under the age of accountability. God at once began to deal with the seven older children, and before long every one of them came to Christ. As the other five grew up they too turned to God, *until the entire twelve were saved!*

I preached this sermon in the Chestnut Street Opera House in Philadelphia. It was broadcast over the air. A mother, in Allentown, Pennsylvania, heard God's voice in the message. She had three grown-up children and a husband. All four were unsaved. She claimed her house for God. Six months later, when Merril T. MacPherson visited Allentown, this mother told him that already her three children were saved and that the husband had started attending church.

A young married woman heard the sermon in the Baptist Temple in Philadelphia, Dr. Russel Conwell's church. Her husband was unsaved. She, also, took God at His word. She thanked God her husband would be saved. I met her ten months later. She and her husband were now active workers in a Presbyterian Church. She said, in her husband's presence, "My husband is before you, a saved man, and a demonstration of the truth of your message." When I think of the glorious possibilities of believing prayer, with this wondrous promise as a basis, I long to go through all the churches of the land, telling God's people of their privilege.

It seems almost too good to be true. It did to a minister of the gospel in Sault Ste. Marie, Canada. I was holding a campaign there and was invited to address the ministerial gathering. I spoke on "Parental Faith." I said that every Christian father held in his hand the destiny of his child. One minister was deeply moved. He was the father of a prodigal son. The boy was away from home. The father carried a burden of anxiety night and day. He prayed for his son. He wept before God. *But he did not actually believe his prayer would be answered.* He was smitten with conviction. God showed him he did not believe. He went home that afternoon and, in his room, he claimed his boy for God. That was on Tuesday. I knew nothing of all this until Friday night when this minister, who was present at the service, told me the above facts. Then he showed me a letter received that day from his son in Windsor, Ontario, nearly three hundred miles away, saying, "Dear Father: On Tuesday I was riding on a train going to Windsor to look for work. God's Spirit came upon me, and I felt I must decide for Christ. I walked through the train looking for a place where I could pray. I found one where the backs of two seats came together. On my face before God, under those seats, I found Christ, and I write to tell you about it."

Blessed be God for this beautiful promise! Blessed be His name for the possibilities of prevailing faith. Blessed be the name of our Lord Jesus Christ, for it is His name that gives efficacy to our prayers. And blessed be the gracious Holy Spirit, by whose convicting power our loved ones are drawn to Christ and saved.

Does it happen that there is an unsaved man or woman reading this message? Have you considered, dear friend, that this wonderful promise is for you? The promise was not given only to the saved. It was addressed to an unsaved man about to send his soul to Hell by way of suicide.

The jailor believed for himself and his household. So may you. Are you a father or a mother? You can be saved and your family with you. It is the grandest thing in life to say "Yes" to God and go to Heaven, taking your children with you. If you say "No" to God, the chances are that your family will say "No" to God, also. Are you willing, after reading this message, to continue without Christ in your life, heading toward the outer darkness, and taking your loved ones with you? If you will bow your head this moment, right where you sit, and with a penitent heart open to Jesus Christ say, "O Lamb of God I come," the Saviour will at once enter. He who died for you will at once come into your heart, never to leave you nor forsake you. Believe this and, because you believe it, thank God for it. Thus you are saved by believing. Then, ask Him to give you faith to believe for your family. He will do so. Go and tell them Christ has come into your heart and that you believe that they too are going to be saved. You will find God is as good as His word. He will not disappoint the faith which He has inspired. "Thou shalt be saved, AND THY HOUSE."

# DWIGHT LYMAN MOODY

∞

Dwight Lyman Moody (1837-1899) may well have been the
greatest evangelist of all time. It was Henry Varley
who said, "It remains to be seen what God will do with a
man who gives himself up wholly to Him" and D.L. Moody resolved
to be, under God, that man. The Encyclopedia Britannica refers to
him as "the greatest of modern evangelists." He founded the
Northfield School for Girls and the Mount Hermon School for boys;
the Northfield Bible College and the famous Moody Bible Institute
in Chicago.

His favourite text was "But he that doeth the will of God abideth
for ever." (I John 2:17). His success as an evangelist was founded
upon his love for the Word of God, his infilling of the Holy Spirit
and his vision for the lost.

In a forty year period he travelled more than a million miles and
preached to more than one hundred million people. Someone asked
him how many people he had seen saved, and he replied "I don't
keep the Lamb's Book of Life."

# Chapter Eleven

# THE WAY OF SALVATION

☙

*Believe on the Lord Jesus Christ, and thou shalt be saved.*
- Acts 16:31

☙

If I say to you, "BELIEVE ON THE LORD JESUS CHRIST," you will reply, "Oh, believer I have heard that word till I am sick and tired of it. Scarcely a week but I hear it in the church, or at a prayer-meeting, or at some meeting." You have all heard it over and over again; I don't suppose there is a child over five years of age but can repeat that text. What you want is to know *how* to believe - what it is to believe.

Some of you say, "We all believe that Christ came into the world to seek and to save the lost; and that he that believeth shalt be saved." But the devils believe, and are not saved. Ay, they believe and tremble! You must believe on the Lord Jesus Christ, and not merely about Him, and then you will know what salvation is.

We will take another word which means the same thing; perhaps you'll get hold of it better: "He came unto his own, and his own receive him not. But as many as received him, to them gave he power to become the sons of God, even to them that believe on his name." Bear in mind, "received him." That's it; not receiving a doctrine or a belief, but receiving Him. It is a person we must receive.

Now, my experience is that we all want to have the power before we receive Christ. That is, we want to feel we are in Christ before we will receive Him. But we cannot love God and feel His presence until we have received Him into our hearts. It is just like a boy with a ball; he throws it to you. You must catch it before you throw it back again. That is the real meaning of "believe" - it is "receive" - receive Christ as yours. I don't know any verse in the Bible that God has blessed to more souls than John 1:12. "To as many as received him, to them gave he power." I don't know any better illustration I could have than matrimony, for every other one doesn't hold good in some points; but I think that is one of the best I could use. Some of you smile at this illustration, but the Bible uses it, and if God uses it in His Word, why should not I? In the Old Testament He uses it - "I am married unto you" (Jeremiah 3:14). Jesus Himself uses it when He speaks of the bride in John 3:29. Paul uses it in his epistles, as in Romans 7:4, as an illustration of the union between Christ and His Church.

Now, it is an illustration you can all understand; there is no one here but knows what it means. When a man offers himself, the woman must do either of two things - either receive or reject him. So every soul must do one of these two things - "receive" or "reject" Christ. If you receive Him, that is all you have to do; He has promised power.

You know that Abraham sent his servant Eliezer a long journey to get a wife for his son Isaac. When Eliezer had got Rebekah, he wanted to be up and off with the young bride; but her mother and brother said, "No, she shall wait awhile." When Eliezer was determined to go, they said, "We will inquire of the damsel." And when Rebekah appeared, they said to her, "Wilt thou go with this man?" That was a crisis in her life. She could not have said "No." Undoubtedly it cost her an effort; it would, of course, be a struggle. She had to give up her parents, home, companions, all that she loved, and go with this stranger. But look at her reply: she said, "I will go." I have come to get a bride for my Master. "Wilt thou go with this man?" I can tell you one thing that Eliezer could not tell Rebekah; he could not say, "Isaac loves you." Isaac had never seen his bride. But I can say, "My Master loves you!"

Ah, that is love! But bear in mind that the moment Rebekah made up her mind to accept Isaac he became everything to her, so that she did not feel she was giving up anything for him. Ah, what a mistake some people make! They say, "I'd like to become a Christian if I hadn't to give up so much." just turn round and look at the other side. You don't have to give up anything - you have simply to receive; and when you have received Christ, everything else vanishes away pretty quickly. Christ fills you, so that you don't feel these things to be worth a thought. When a woman marries a man, it is generally love that prompts her. If any one is here that really loves a man, is she thinking of how much she will have to give up? No - that wouldn't be love. Love doesn't feed upon itself, it feeds upon the person who is loved. It is not by looking at what you will have to give up but by looking at what you will receive that you will be enabled to accept the Saviour. What is He willing to be to you, if you will have Him? Won't you be made heirs of heaven, joint-heirs with Christ, to reign with Him forever and ever, to be His, to be with Him where He is, to be what He is? Think, then, of what He is, and of what He gives. You don't need to trouble yourselves at present about what you have to give up. Receive Him, and all these things will appear utterly insignificant.

I used to think of what I would have to give up. I dearly loved many of the pleasures of this earth, but now I'd as soon go out into your streets and eat dirt as do those things. God does not say, "Give up this and that." He says, "Here is the Son of my bosom - receive Him." When you do receive Him, everything else goes. Stop that talk about giving up; let Christ save you, and all these things will go for nothing. Mark the words, "To as many as received him, to them gave he power." Now, will you go with this man? You have often heard about Christ; you know as much about Him as any one on this platform, perhaps; but did you ever know a man or woman who regretted receiving Him? No man ever regretted receiving Christ; but I have heard thousands who have been followers of the devil, and have regretted it bitterly. And I notice that it is always the most faithful followers of the devil who regret it most.

Now, another case - Ruth and Orpah. Many are like these two young widows. A crisis had come in their lives; they had lost their husbands, and had been living up there in the mountains of Moab. Often had they visited the graves of their dear ones, and perhaps planted a few flowers there, and watered them with their tears. Now, Naomi is about to return to her native land, and they think they will go a bit of the road with her. It is a sad parting; but now the crisis comes. Down in the valley they embrace each other, and give the parting kiss. Then they both say they will go with Naomi, but she warns them of the difficulties and the trials which might await them. So Orpah says, "I will go back to my people"; but Ruth cannot leave her mother-in-law, and says she will go with her. Orpah turns back alone, and I can see her on the top of the hill; she stops, and turns round for a last look. And Naomi says to Ruth. "Behold, thy sister-in-law is gone back to her people, and unto her gods; return thou after thy sister-in-law." What does Ruth say? "Entreat me not to leave thee, or to return from following after thee; for whither thou goest, I will go; and where thou lodgest, I will lodge; thy people shall be my people, and thy God my God." Her choice was made. Poverty here or suffering and want yonder, she would share Naomi's lot.

Orpah loved Naomi, but not enough to leave all for her; while Ruth loved her mother-in-law so much that the leaving of her people seemed nothing to her. Oh, may God draw out all your hearts, so that you may leave all and follow Him! We never hear any more of Orpah; the curtain falls upon her life. Perhaps she died away up in the mountains of Moab, without God and without hope. But how different with Ruth! She becomes famous in history; she is one of the few women whose names have come along down the roll of ages; and she is brought into the royal line of heaven. I have an idea that God blessed her for that decision. And He will bless you if you decide in a like manner. Will you say as Ruth did, "I will follow thee; and thy God shall be my God"? Will any one take up the language of Ruth? Is there not a Ruth here? If there is, the Master is calling.

I'll take another word. I have been speaking of "receive" - the next word I want your attention to is "trusting." Many get hold of that when they cannot get hold of "believe" or "receive." You all know what it is to trust. If it were not for trust, there would be a terrible commotion in this building tonight. If you could not trust that the roof was firmly put up, you would get out pretty quickly; and if you could not trust these chairs to support you, how long would you sit on them? Why, you wouldn't have come here at all if you didn't trust our word that there would be an address. Now, it is just the same trust that God wants. It is no miraculous trust or faith, but just the same kind, only the object is different. Instead of trusting in these earthly things, or in an arm of flesh, you are asked to trust in the Son of God.

In Dublin I was speaking to a lady in the inquiry room, when I noticed a gentleman walking up and down before the door. I went forward and said, "Are you a Christian?" He was very angry, and turned on his heel and left me. The following Sunday night I was preaching about "receiving," and I put the question, "Who'll receive Him now?" That young man was present, and the question sank into his heart. The next day he called upon me, he was a merchant in that city, and he said, "Do you remember me?" "No, I don't." "Do you remember the young man who answered you so roughly the other night?" "Yes, I do." "Well, I've come to tell you I am saved." "How did it happen?" "Why, I was listening to your sermon last night, and when you asked, 'Who'll receive Him now?' God put it into my heart to say, 'I will'; and He has opened my eyes to see His Son now." I don't know why thousands should not do that here tonight. If you are ever to be saved, why not now?

But another point you must remember - salvation is a free gift, and it is a free gift for all. Can you buy it? It is a free gift, presented to "whosoever . . ." Suppose I were to say, I will give this Bible to "whosoever . . ." what have you got to do? Why, nothing but take it. But a man comes forward and says, "I'd like that Bible very much." "Well, didn't I say 'whosoever'...?" "Yes; but I'd like to have you say my name." "Well, here it is." Still he keeps eyeing the Bible, and saying, "I'd like to have that Bible; but I'd like to give you something for it. I don't like to take it for nothing." "Well, I am not here to sell Bibles: take it, if you want it." "Well, I want it; but I'd like to give you something for it. Let me give you a penny for it; though, to be sure, it's worth twenty or thirty dollars." Well, suppose I took the penny; the man takes up the Bible, and marches away home with it. His wife says, "Where did you get that Bible?" "Oh, I bought it." Mark the point; when he gives the penny it ceases to be a gift. So with salvation. If you were to pay ever so little, it would not be a gift.

Man is always trying to do something. This miserable word "try" is keeping thousands out of heaven. When I hear men speak of "trying," I generally tell them it is the way down to death and hell. I believe more souls are lost through "trying" than any other way. You have often tried, and as often failed; and as long as you keep trying you will fail. Drop that word, then, and take as your sure foothold for eternity, "trust." "Though he slay me, yet will I trust him"; that is the right kind of trust. Would to God that you would all say, "I will trust Him now, tonight." Did you ever hear of any one going down to hell trusting in Jesus? I never did. This very night, if you commit yourself to Him, the battle will be over.

You complain you don't feel better. Well, remember, the child must be born before it can be taught. So we cannot learn of God until we receive Him. We must be born - born again ere we can feel. Christ must be in us the hope of glory. How can He be in us if we don't receive Him and trust Him?

Another verse on which I feel that I rest my own salvation is John 5:24. I trust God will write it on your hearts, and burn it down into your souls. "Verily, verily, I say unto you, He that heareth my word, and believeth on him that sent me, hath everlasting life." Thank God for that "hath."

I had a few men in the inquiry room one night who could not find peace. I said, "Do you believe the Bible?" "Yes, sir." "I think I will prove you don't. Turn up John 5:24." They turned it up. "Read the verse." "He that heareth my word," "You believe that?" "Yes sir." "And believeth on him that sent me" "You believe that God sent Jesus?" "Yes." "Well, read on." "Hath everlasting life." "You believe you have everlasting life?" "No, we don't." "Oh, I thought you didn't believe in the Bible!" What right have you to cut a verse in two, and say you believe the one half but not the other? It plainly says that he who believes "hath everlasting life, and shall not come into condemnation; but is passed from death unto life." Why, if you believe God's words, you can say, "I have passed from darkness into light." just by resting on that one little word in the present tense we may have "assurance" now. We don't need to wait till we die, and till the great day of judgment, to find it out.

A lady in Glasgow came to me, and said, "Mr. Moody, you are always saying, 'Take, take!' Is there any place in the Bible where it says 'Take,' or is it only a word you use? I have been looking in the Bible for it, but cannot see it." "Why," I said, "the Bible is sealed with it; it is almost the last word in the Bible. 'And the Spirit and the bride say, Come. And let him that heareth say, Come. And let him that is athirst come. And whosoever will, let him take the water of life freely.'" "Well," she said, "I never saw that before. Is that all I have to do?" "Yes, the Bible says so." And she took it, just there. God says, "Let him take"; who can stop us if God says it? All the devils in hell cannot hinder a poor soul from taking if God says, "Take." My friends, are you going to "take"? Are you going to let these precious meetings pass without getting Christ - without being able to look up and say, "Christ is my Saviour, God is my Father, heaven is my home."

A lady came to my house one night, anxious about her soul; but after some conversation she left, without finding peace. She came again, and I asked, "What is the trouble?" "I haven't got peace." I took her to this verse, "He that believeth on the Son hath everlasting life" (John 3:36) I just held up that little word "hath" to her, and turned to John 5:24 and 6:47. There these words were spoken by Jesus, and they are all linked on to believing on the Son. After we had talked for some time, she looked in my face earnestly, and said, "I have got it!" and went away rejoicing in the Saviour's love. If you seek life you can have it now, as you sit upon your seat. The word "hath" occurs again in Isaiah 53:60: "All we like sheep have gone astray; . . . and the Lord hath laid on him the iniquity of us all." Our iniquity has been laid upon Christ, and the Lord is not going to demand payment twice. "Who his own self bare our sins in his own body on the tree."

Now, one question: What are you going to do with Christ? You have got to settle that question. You may get angry, but you must settle it. Pilate wanted to shirk the responsibility, and sent Jesus to Herod; but he was forced to a decision. When the Jews forced him to decide, he washed his hands, and said he was "innocent of this just man's blood." But did that take away his guilt? No.

An angel may be here, hovering over this audience, and he is listening to what is said. Some one may say, "I will receive Him; I will delay no longer." Immediately the angel will wing his way right up to the pearly gates, and tells the news that another sinner has been saved. There will be a new song ringing through the courts of heaven over sinners repenting. God will issue the command to write down their names in the book of life, and to get rooms ready for them in the new Jerusalem, where we all will soon be.

A man was being tried for a crime, the punishment of which was death. The witnesses came in one by one, and testified to his guilt, but there he stood quite calm and unmoved. The judge and the jury were quite surprised at his indifference; they could not understand how he could take such a serious matter so calmly. When the jury retired, it did not take them many minutes to decide on the verdict, "guilty"; and when the judge was passing the sentence of death upon the criminal, he told him how surprised he was that he could be so unmoved by the prospect of death. When the judge had finished, the man put his hand in his bosom, pulled out a document, and walked out of the dock a free man. Ah, that was why he could be so calm; it was a free pardon from his king, which he had hid in his pocket all the time. The king had instructed him to allow the trial to proceed, and to produce the pardon only when he was condemned. No wonder, then, that he was indifferent as to the result of the trial. Now, that is just what will make us joyful in the great day of judgment; we have got a pardon from the Great King, and it is sealed with the blood of His Son.

After the Chicago fire, a great many things were sent to us from all parts of the world. The boxes they came in were labelled "For the people who were burned out," and all a man had to do was to prove that he had been burned out, and he got a share. So you have but to prove that you are poor, miserable sinners, and there's help for you. If every man who is ruined and lost will cling to "try" there is no hope; but if he gives it all up as a bad job, then Christ will save him. The law condemns us, but Christ saves us.

The superintendent of a Sabbath school was walking down the street one day, when he met a policeman leading by the hand a little boy, who was crying bitterly. He stopped, and asked the policeman what was the matter with the boy. "Oh," said the officer, "he is lost." The superintendent asked to look at him. They went to a lamp, and held up the little fellow. Why, in a moment the boy knew his superintendent, and flew to his arms. The gentleman took him from the policeman, and the boy was comforted. The law has got us, but let us flee into Jesus' arms, and we are safe.

A friend of mine in the North told me of a poor Scottish lassie, who was very anxious about her soul. He told her to read Isaiah 53. She replied, "I canna read, and I canna pray; Jesus, take me as I am!" That was the true way; and Jesus just took her as she was. Let Him take you, just as you are, and He will receive you to His arms.

One night, when preaching in Philadelphia, right down by the side of the pulpit there was a young lady, whose eyes were riveted on me as if she were drinking in every word. It is precious to preach to people like that; they generally get good, even if the sermon is poor. I got interested in her, and after I had done talking, I went and spoke to her. "Are you a Christian?" "No, I wish I was; I have been seeking Jesus for three years." I said, "There must be some mistake." She looked strangely at me, and said, "Don't you believe me?" "Well, no doubt you thought you were seeking Jesus; but it doesn't take an anxious sinner three years to meet an anxious Saviour." "What am I to do, then?" "The matter is, you are trying to do something; you must just believe on the Lord Jesus Christ." "Oh, I am sick and tired of the word, 'Believe, believe, believe!' I don't know what it is." "Well," I said, "we'll change the word; take 'trust.' " "If I say, 'I'll trust Him,' will He save me?" "No, I don't say that; you may say a thousand things, but if you do trust Him." "Well," she said, "I do trust Him; but," she added in the same breath, "I don't feel any better." "Ah, I've got it now! You've been looking for feelings for three years instead of for Jesus. Faith is up above, not down here."

People are always looking for feelings. You are getting up a new translation of the Bible here, and if the men who are translating it would only put in feelings instead of faith, what a rush there would be for that Bible. But if you look from Genesis to Revelation, you cannot find feelings attached to salvation. We must rise above feelings; if you could, what a time you'd have! I know I would never have the toothache or the headache.

"Feelings," is the last plank the devil sticks out, just as your feet are getting on the "Rock of Ages." Some sermons you have heard arouse you, but then you feel all right when you get on this plank. Six months after, perhaps you are dying, and the devil comes along when you think you are quite safe. "Ah," he tells you, "that was my work; I made you feel good." And where are you then? Oh, take your stand on God's Word, then you cannot fail. His Word has been tried for six thousand years, and it has not failed.

So I said to the lady, "Have no more to do with feelings; but, like Job, say, 'Though he slay me, yet will I trust him.'" She looked at me a few minutes, and then, putting out her hand to take mine, she said, "Mr. Moody, I trust the Lord Jesus Christ to save my soul tonight." Then she went to the elders and said the same words. As she passed out she met one of the church officers, and, shaking his hand, said again, "I trust the Lord Jesus to save my soul."

Next night she was right before me again. I shall never forget her beaming face; the light of eternity was shining in her eyes! She went into the inquiry-room. I wondered what she was going there for; but when I got there, I found her with her arms around a lady friend, saying, "It's only to trust Him. I have found it so." From that night she was one of the best workers in the inquiry-room, and whenever I met a difficult case, I got her to speak to the person, and she was sure to help the person.

Surely you can trust God. You must have a very poor opinion of God if you cannot trust Him. You have only to come to Him thus - receive Him, trust Him. What more can you do, and what less can you do than trust Him? Is He not worthy of it? Now, let us be perfectly still a moment, and while the voice of man is hushed, let us think of one passage of Scripture: "Behold, I stand at the door and knock." That is Christ standing at the door of your heart, knocking, and He says, "If any man hear my voice, and open the door, I will come unto him, and will sup with him, and he with me." Will any one pull back the bolts, and say, "Enter, thou welcome, thrice welcome One. Blessed Saviour, come in." God grant that all of us may do this!

# ROBERT MURRAY McCHEYNE

Robert Murray McCheyne was born in Scotland in 1813. When he was just four years of age and recovering from an illness he taught himself how to write the Greek alphabet. A young man of great intellect, he attended the University of Edinburgh graduating in 1830. At the age of twenty-two he was licensed to preach and a year later he was ordained and became the minister of St. Peter's Church of Scotland in Dundee. He pastored the church for six years and during that period the membership grew to over one thousand.

In 1839 he visited Palestine and while he was there he prayed faithfully for his congregation back home. When he returned to Scotland he discovered that a spiritual awakening was in progress and his continued fervent preaching was instrumental in the revival reaching across Scotland and into England.

The secret of his power in preaching is contained in the advice he gave to one of his ministerial brethren.

'Get your text from God - your thoughts, your words from God.'

'It is not great talents God blesses so much as likeness to Jesus.'

'A holy minister is an awful weapon in the hand of God.'

McCheyne lived a short but useful life, labouring for the salvation of souls, and although he left notes of only 300 sermons when he died in 1843, he belongs to that class of preachers whose sermons should always be in print.

His sermon on the conversion of Lydia and the Philippian jailor brings before us those tender pleadings with sinners as he sought to win them for Christ.

# Chapter Twelve

# LYDIA AND THE JAILOR

⌇

*And from thence to Philippi, which is the chief city of that part of
Macedonia, and a colony: and we were in that city abiding certain
days. And on the Sabbath we went out of the city by a riverside,
where prayer was wont to be made; and we sat down, and spake
unto the women which resorted thither. And a certain woman
named Lydia, a seller of purple, of the city of Thyatira, which
worshipped God, heard us: whose heart the Lord opened, that she
attended unto the things which were spoken of Paul.*
*And when she was baptized, and her household, she besought us,
saying, If ye have judged me to be faithful to the Lord, come into
my house, and abide there. And she constrained us. And it came to
pass, as we went to prayer, a certain damsel possessed with a
spirit of divination met us, which brought her masters much gain
by soothsaying: The same followed Paul and us, and cried,
saying, These men are the servants of the most high God, which
shew unto us the way of salvation.*
*And this did she many days. But Paul, being grieved, turned and
said to the spirit, I command thee in the name of Jesus Christ to
come out of her. And he came out the same hour. And when her
masters saw that the hope of their gains was gone, they caught
Paul and Silas, and drew them into the marketplace unto the
rulers, And brought them to the magistrates, saying, These men,
being Jews, do exceedingly trouble our city. And teach customs,
which are not lawful for us to receive, neither to observe, being
Romans.*

*And the multitude rose up together against them: and the
magistrates rent off their clothes, and commanded to beat them.
And when they had laid many stripes upon them, they cast them
into prison, charging the jailor to keep them safely:
Who, having received such a charge, thrust them into the inner
prison, and made their feet fast in the stocks.
And at midnight Paul and Silas prayed, and sang praises unto
God and the prisoners heard them.   And suddenly there was a
great earthquake, so that the foundations of the prison were
shaken: and immediately all the doors were opened, and every
one's bands were loosed.   And the keeper of the prison awaking
out of his sleep, and seeing the prison doors open, he drew out his
sword, and would have killed himself, supposing that the prisoners
had been fled.   But Paul cried with a loud voice, saying, Do
thyself no harm: for we are all here.   Then he called for a light,
and sprang in, and came trembling, and fell down before Paul and
Silas. And brought them out, and said, Sirs, what must I do to be
saved?   And they said, Believe on the Lord Jesus Christ, and thou
shalt be saved, and thy house.   And they spake unto him the word
of the Lord, and to all that were in his house.   And he took them
the same hour of the night, and washed their stripes; and was
baptized, he and all his, straightway.   And when he had brought
them into his house, he set meat before them, and rejoiced,
believing in God with all his house. And when it was day, the
magistrates sent the serjeants, saying, Let those men go. And the
keeper of the prison told this saying to Paul, The magistrates have
sent to let you go: now therefore depart, and go in peace.*
- Acts 16:12-36

ᏸ

And from thence to Philippi, which is the chief city of that part of
Macedonia, *and* a colony: and we were in that city abiding certain
days.  And on the sabbath we went out of the city by a river side,
where prayer was wont to be made; and we sat down, and spake
unto the women which resorted *thither.*  And a certain woman named

Lydia, a seller of purple, of the city of Thyatira, which worshipped God, heard us: whose heart the Lord opened, that she attended unto the things which were spoken of Paul. And when she was baptized, and her household, she besought us, saying, If ye have judged me to be faithful to the Lord, come into my house, and abide *there*. And she constrained us. And it came to pass, as we went to prayer, a certain damsel possessed with a spirit of divination met us, which brought her masters much gain by soothsaying: The same followed Paul and us, and cried, saying, These men are the servants of the most high God, which shew unto us the way of salvation. And this did she many days. But Paul, being grieved, turned and said to the spirit, I command thee in the name of Jesus Christ to come out of her; And he came out the same hour. And when her masters saw that the hope of their gains was gone, they caught Paul and Silas, and drew *them* into the marketplace unto the rulers, and brought them to the magistrates, saying, These men, being Jews, do exceedingly trouble our city, and teach customs, which are not lawful for us to receive, neither to observe, being Romans. And the multitude rose up together against them: and the magistrates rent off their clothes, and commanded to beat *them*. And when they had laid many stripes upon them, they cast *them* into prison, charging the jailor to keep them safely: Who, having received such a charge, thrust them into the inner prison, and made their feet fast in the stocks. And at midnight Paul and Silas prayed, and sang praises unto God: and the prisoners heard them. And suddenly there was a great earthquake, so that the foundations of the prison were shaken: and immediately all the doors were opened, and every one's bands were loosed. And the keeper of the prison awaking out of his sleep, and seeing the prison doors open, he drew out his sword, and would have killed himself, supposing that the prisoners had been fled. But Paul cried with a loud voice, saying, Do thyself no harm: for we are all here. Then he called for a light, and sprang in, and came trembling, and fell down before Paul and Silas, and brought them out, and said, Sirs, what must I do to be saved? And they said, Believe on the Lord Jesus Christ, and thou shalt be saved, and thy house. And they spake unto him the word of the Lord, and to all that were in his house. And he took them the same hour of the night, and washed their stripes; and was baptized, he and all his, straightway. And when he had brought them into his house, he set meat before them, and rejoiced, believing in God with all his house. And when it was day, the magistrates sent the sergeants, saying, Let those men go. And the keeper of the prison told this saying to Paul, The magistrates have sent to let you go: now therefore depart, and go in peace.

God's ways are not like our ways, neither are his thoughts like our thoughts. When God sent Paul the vision of a man of Macedonia praying him and saying, 'Come over and help us?' Who would have guessed that Lydia the seller of purple and the heathen jailor of Philippi were to be the first-fruits of Macedonia unto Christ? Or when these apostolic men hearing the commission, 'Go ye into all the world and preach the gospel to every creature', entered the gates of Philippi, a Roman colony, and the chief city of that part of Macedonia, who would have guessed that the homes of Lydia and the house of the jailor were the only two marked out by God for a blessing?

*Lydia,* we find, was a seller of purple from Thyatira, a city of Asia Minor, who had settled in Philippi, as we find she had a house and a household. That she was a Jewess or at least a Jewish proselyte is evident from her being one of those women who on the Sabbath day resorted to a place by the riverside for prayer. And it is said she worshipped God. She was then by no means a profligate or profane woman but one who waited on the Jewish ordinance of prayer - and yet she was unconverted. Oh, my friends, how many of you who, like Lydia, are far from being profligate or profane, how many of you who live honest and respectable lives, who wait on the ordinances of God and mingle with the worshippers of God, are yet, like Lydia, unconverted and need, like Lydia, to have your hearts opened by God to receive the truth of the love of God?

*The jailor* again was evidently a heathen man whose dark mind had never been enlightened by the knowledge of God or the promise of the Saviour. A man of force and of cruelty. The cruelty of his disposition is particularly remarkable in that when he was charged to keep them safely, he made that an excuse for keeping them cruelly. He *thrust* them into the inner prison. He might have kept them safely without thrusting them in. And not only so but as if the innermost prison were not sufficient to hold them fast, he made their feet fast in the stocks.

Such were the two whom God chose to be the firstfruits of Macedonia, a formalist professor and a hard-hearted heathen. How true the saying that is written, 'Many are called, but few are chosen.' Paul and his companions were many days in that city and no doubt preached the gospel to all that would listen. But we are only told of two houses where the hearts were opened, two of the most unlikely perhaps in the whole place, a foreign woman and a heathen jailor.

As it was then, so it is now: 'Many are called, but few are chosen.' We come this day with the message to all. There is not one of your houses that we are not anxious to enter with the message of salvation; there is not a man, woman or child to whom we do not this day offer Christ. Yea, there is not one of you, however dead and formal in your religiousness, however ignorant and cruel and profane, of whom the Lord permits us to despair. We know not to which one of you the Lord may this very hour bring the message, opening your heart to attend to the things that are spoken. To one and all do we this day anew offer Christ and all his benefits. We bring in the blood of Jesus and the righteousness of Jesus, a full and free salvation, and we lay all down at your feet. And we invite everyone to take Christ and have life as we say, 'Why will ye die?' Yea, and if you can tell me any way by which we can get at your hearts with greater plainness and power, we are ready to take that way of laying Christ before you. But will you all accept? Will all your hearts be opened? Will you all go back to your houses changed men, rejoicing in the free forgiveness of sins as those who have found great spoil? Alas, no! God will act differently from His normal way of dealing if he does so. For though He wishes you all to be saved and has no pleasure that one man, woman or child should perish, yet He tells us plainly that we are not to expect that the many will listen to us. He tells us that most of you will go on in your hardness, one going to his farm and another to his merchandise, that the most of you will hear and wonder and perish. And if He this day open the heart of some poor Lydia among you, some stranger whom you know not of and care not for, or if He bring some stout-hearted cruel man to cry out, 'What must I do to be saved?', this is all the reward that He bids us expect for our pains.

Let us now attempt briefly to trace the different steps in conversion as they are shown us in the conversion of the jailor, which is the fullest of the two. Conversion is always the same work and though there are many differences in time, place and circumstances, yet the main features of all conversions are the same:

## 1. Conviction of being a lost sinner is the first feature in this conversion

And it is the first feature in all true conversions. We find that Paul and Silas, though their backs were furrowed with stripes, and though thrust into the innermost dungeon, with their feet made fast in the stocks, yet at midnight prayed and sang praises unto God. Being afflicted they prayed, yet being merry they sang psalms. The black dungeon walls of that heathen prison-house, that had till now resounded only with the cries and groans of the prisoner, or the still more hideous grating of heathen oaths and profaneness, now resounded through all its vaults for the first time with the praises of Jesus. And the prisoners heard them and suddenly, as a token that their prayers were heard and their praise accepted, there was a great earthquake so that the foundations of the prison were shaken and immediately all the doors were opened and everyone's bonds were loosed. And the keeper of the prison awaking out of his sleep and seeing the prison doors open, drew out his sword and would have killed himself supposing that the prisoners had fled. But Paul cried with a loud voice, 'Do thyself no harm, for we are all here.' Then it was that the work of grace was begun in this hard-hearted man.

What was the exact train of thought that brought him to the conviction of sin, it may be hard to explain. The prison doors being thus wonderfully opened may have convinced him that God was on the side of these men; their patience in suffering and their calmness in their hour of danger also convinced him that God was in them of a truth. His own harsh treatment of the servants of the Most High God, his ignorance of that God, how he had been fighting against

God, and how near he had rushed by his own hand into hell, all this seems to have flashed across his mind and to have awakened the complete conviction that he was a lost sinner. For he called for a light, and sprang in and came trembling and fell down at the feet of Paul and Silas and brought them out and said, *'Sirs, what must I do to be saved?'*

My dear friends, have you ever asked this question, 'What must I do to be saved?' Not with the lips only but with the heart. Have you ever asked it with the intense anxiety of one who could not rest without an answer? Have you ever asked, as the Jews did, the way to Zion with their faces thitherward? Oh my friends, if you have never had any bosom-anxiety upon this subject, then you have never been convinced of sin, and it is all in vain that we preach Jesus to you. You can see no sense in a Saviour, for you do not feel any danger from which you are to be saved. Then the work of grace hath never been begun in your heart and you are as far from the kingdom of God as it is possible for any man to be who is not in hell.

Let us stir you up, if it be possible, to ask this question now, 'Did you ever think or believe that if you had no more than one sin you would be worthy of hell?' You know that God is a being of infinite loveliness and beauty, all perfection dwells in Him. Whatever is lovely or amiable in any creature dwells infinitely in God. But the more amiable any object is, the more are we under obligation to love that object. We are more under obligation to love the children of God than the children of the world, for they are far more amiable and worthy of our love. But God is infinitely amiable or infinitely worthy of our love, therefore we are under infinite obligation to love Him. And if we do not love Him, then we are breaking an infinite obligation.

But every sin we commit proves that we do not love God, for if we loved Him we would love to do His will. Therefore every sin is breaking an infinite obligation and, therefore, every sin deserves an infinite punishment. But an infinite punishment is hell. Therefore every sin deserves hell. Suppose then that there were but one sin lying on you; that one sin, my friend, is heavy enough to sink you to the lowest hell, and angels and men and devils and your own conscience would be found to say it was just and right it should be so. Just as one millstone tied round the neck will sink you to the bottom of the sea, so one unpardoned sin lying on your conscience is enough to sink you to the depths of hell.

But oh, my friends, is there no more than one unpardoned sin lying on you? Is not every faculty of your nature perverted by sin? The whole head is sick and the whole heart is faint. Is not your judgement perverted by sin? Do you not call good evil and evil good? Do you not put sweet for bitter and bitter for sweet? Is not your memory perverted by sin? How easily you can store up anything that will do the devil service in your heart. What a memory you have for worldly business or worldly pleasures, but you have no memory for the things of God, for the Word of God. Is not your imagination perverted? Is not every imagination of your heart only evil and that continually? How constantly have you abused that noble faculty to serve the basest sins. What a sick fancy you have for calling up scenes of folly and pollution and wickedness. What horrid imaginations crowd through your mind in the night watches. And then is not your heart perverted? Have you not loved the creature more than the Creator who is blessed for evermore? Have you not thrown away your best affections upon things that perish in the very using? And when you have been brought off from one object of your affection, has not your heart just given away after another as vain and vile and contemptible?

Look back over the history of your affections. Oh, what a scene of mad idolatry. Does it not show to you, as poor and contemptible as that of the Hindu that worships wood and stone, that the only Being in the Universe worthy of your supreme love has been trodden under foot. Truly the whole head is sick and the whole heart faint, from the sole of the foot to the crown of the head; there is no soundness in you but wounds and bruises and putrefying sores. Think then what mountains of sin are lying on you. It is not one sin that hangs like a millstone about your neck but whole mountains of sin are piled over you, more than the hairs of your head in number, all crushing you down to the lowest hell. And there is nothing between you and that place of woe but the thin thread of life which may be snapped by the scissors of disease in one night.

It is quite true you do not feel this load. You do not feel a featherweight upon your soul, you are not like men who have a burden on their backs.  But that makes your case all the more horrible and dangerous.  Just as the sick man's case is all the more dangerous if he does not feel that anything ails him, just as the slaves were all the more hopeless slaves because they did not feel the weight of slavery, so your case is all the more dangerous and terrible because you do not feel the weight of God's wrath that is pressing upon you.  There are mountains of sin upon you, yet you feel them not.  Oh, will none of you awake to feel the reality?  Will none of you be alarmed by the awful burden of the Almighty's wrath?  Will none of you be persuaded to cry out, 'Sirs, what must I do to be saved?'  Oh, if we could get one of you to have a true sense of your sin, of the weight that is abiding on every Christless soul, I know well for I have seen it, how quickly you would run, trembling like the jailor, to ask of the weakest child of God, 'What must I do to be saved?'

## 2. But I hasten, secondly, to the answer of the apostles

This awakened the second grand conviction in his soul, the conviction of righteousness (vs.31-32).

To the awakened soul asking, What must I do to be saved? The gospel is the simplest of all contrivances that any mind could have imagined.  To a soul that really feels mountains of unpardoned sin lying upon it; to a soul that feels that nothing he can do, no prayers, no tears, no works of penance can ever lift off the burden; to a soul that is really emptied of all self, of struggles, who says as one poor soul did, 'It is done, it is done, I never can do anything to save myself;' to that soul nothing can be plainer, simpler, more apt and fitting, than the offer of Jesus to bear the whole load, to suffer the whole curse.  The soul slips from under the oppressive mountain and leaves it weighing down upon the shoulder of the almighty Redeemer.  For it is written, 'On him were laid the iniquities of us all.'  The soul chooses Christ as a sin-bearer, cleaves to him, and is at peace for eternity.

But there are many of you to whom the answer of the apostle is utter foolishness.  There are many of you who attach no meaning to the words, 'Believe on the Lord Jesus Christ....'  There are many of you who would have given the jailor a very different answer.  You would have said, 'Be an honest man, put away drunkenness and swearing and cruelty; live decently and respectably in the world and so you will be saved?' Or at least there are many of you who, if you were honest, must frankly confess that you do not see how believing on Jesus would save the man.

Another consequence of conversion here given us is love and hospitality to the saints. It was thus with Lydia (v.15) and it was thus with the hard-hearted jailor. That same night he was cruel and harsh to them: thrust them into the inner prison; put their feet in the stocks, nay he was cruel to himself and his wife and children for he drew his sword and would have killed himself. But he is now a believer in Jesus, the lion is turned into the lamb: 'he took them the same hour of the night, and washed their stripes...' (v.33).

This is a sure and unfailing feature of the children of God. Examine yourselves by it, I beseech you. If you be of the unconverted world, you will have one of two characters: either you will be covetous and greedy and grasping and hoarding and hard-handed and never running the least risk of entertaining angels unawares; or else your profuse hospitality and gentlemanly generosity will be poured out alike upon the pious and the profane.

But if you be the children of God, your hospitality and your charity will be quite different. You will have bowels of compassion for the unconverted world as Jesus had, who loved them and gave himself for them. But the bosom friends of your heart will be the children of God. Toward them you will show hospitality indeed without judging. When they are naked you will clothe them; when they are hungry you will feed them; when they are sick and in prison you will visit them; for you know that inasmuch as you do it unto the least of these Christ's brethren you do it unto Christ. Yea, you will give even a cup of cold water with peculiar joy to a disciple because he is a disciple of Jesus, and you shall in no wise lose your reward.

*In conclusion*

I return to what I said at first, that many are called but few are chosen. We this day call to every one of you. We have laid before you the reason why you should flee from the wrath to come - because of the mountains of sin that are lying on you. We have laid before you the completeness and all-sufficiency of Christ to bear all that load. And there is not one of you too cold, too hard, too careless that we despair of your conversion this day. May the Lord grant that some poor formalist like Lydia may have her heart opened, that some cruel man like the jailor may be brought to cry, 'What must I do to be saved?' And so God shall have all the praise in time and in eternity!

*29th June 1836, preached in Barrowhall*
*3rd July 1836, preached in Dunipace*
*4th July 1836, preached at Blackmill Canon*
*1836, preached in St. Peter's*

**Other titles written / compiled by
Stanley Barnes include:**

All For Jesus – The Life of W. P. Nicholson

Goodbye God - Stirring Messages by W. P. Nicholson

An Inspirational Treasury of D. L. Moody

An Inspirational Treasury of Samuel Rutherford

God Makes A Path – A Devotional from the Writings of
R. M. McCheyne

Sermons on John 3:16

Sermons on Isaiah 63

Visit our web site for updates
**www.ambassador-productions.com**